CHASING EASY
in a Life of
HARD CHOICES

CHASING EASY
in a Life of
HARD CHOICES

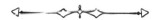

*Failed Marriages, Unplanned Pregnancies
and the God Who Restores*

TERESA LEET

XULON PRESS ELITE

Xulon Press Elite
2301 Lucien Way #415
Maitland, FL 32751
407.339.4217
www.xulonpress.com

© 2021 by Teresa Leet

Special Thanks To:
Gleniece Lytle, Desert Rain Editing
Kym McDowell

All rights reserved solely by the author. The author guarantees all contents are original and do not infringe upon the legal rights of any other person or work. No part of this book may be reproduced in any form without the permission of the author.

Due to the changing nature of the Internet, if there are any web addresses, links, or URLs included in this manuscript, these may have been altered and may no longer be accessible. The views and opinions shared in this book belong solely to the author and do not necessarily reflect those of the publisher. The publisher therefore disclaims responsibility for the views or opinions expressed within the work.

Unless otherwise indicated, Scripture quotations taken from the Holy Bible, New Living Translation (NLT). Copyright ©1996, 2004, 2007 by Tyndale House Foundation. Used by permission of Tyndale House Publishers, Inc.

Scripture quotations taken from the Holy Bible, New International Version (NIV). Copyright © 1973, 1978, 1984, 2011 by Biblica, Inc.™. Used by permission. All rights reserved.

Paperback ISBN-13: 978-1-6628-1884-4

Ebook ISBN-13: 978-1-6628-1885-1

This book is dedicated to those who feel their past prevents them from God's promises of an abundant life in the future.

If God cares so wonderfully for wildflowers that are here today and thrown into the fire tomorrow, He will certainly care for you.
—Matthew 6:30 (NEW LIVING TRANSLATION)

Life is easy, it's the choices you make that are hard.
—*Ron Leet, Jr.*

Table of Contents

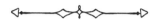

Foreword xi
Introduction xiii

Part 1: Toxic Relationships and the Tragedy of Abortion

Chapter 1: The Egg and the Gift of Manure 1
Chapter 2: You Always Remember Your First 9
Chapter 3: The Barbarism of Late-Term Abortion 25
Chapter 4: Love Equals Validation 37
Chapter 5: From Broken to Bride 41
Chapter 6: The Masquerade Charade 49

Part 2: Adoption and Redemption

Chapter 7: The Foundation of Faith 69
Chapter 8: When His Love Found Me 75
Chapter 9: Make God Choices, Not Just Good Choices 85
Chapter 10: A Whispering Butterfly and Wind on a Buttercup ... 99
Chapter 11: Information Trumps Ignorance 113
Chapter 12: Sweet Redemption and Refreshing Restoration .. 123
Chapter 13: Finishing the Work Assigned to Me 139

Part 3: Knowledge and Perspective

Chapter 14: It's Reigning Men 155
Chapter 15: Silent Witnesses—The Butterfly Effect 163
Conclusion: A Love Letter From Your Heavenly Father 169

Acknowledgments. 173
Resources 175
About the Author. 187
Endnotes 189

Foreword

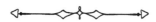

It is my privilege to introduce you to my friend, Teresa Leet. I first met Teresa and her husband, Ron, in a leadership development program at our church. My first thought in meeting her was, "This woman is a tenacious straight-shooter! She is after God's best for her life, and she doesn't play!" Within moments of meeting Teresa, I believe you also would pick up on her genuine desire to add value to people.

I have personally witnessed her push past the threshold of fear in many areas of her life. Teresa lives with a deep conviction that real people are waiting on the other side of her obedience. She is right.

Teresa saw you reading the manuscript of her soul long before this book was ever created. She envisioned people benefiting from the compound interest of her pain and walking away with time-tested wisdom.

In *Chasing Easy in a Life of Hard Choices*, welcome to the school of hard knocks. We get the privilege of reading about it, while Teresa paid a high price to live it: 42 years of pain, loss, and learning. Emerging as anything but a powerless victim, Teresa offers each of us a path to hope. She shines much-needed light on the path to an empowered life. A life covered in undeniable grace and yet dependent on sustainable grit.

Leadership guru, John Maxwell, once said that experience is not the greatest teacher but evaluated experience is. Evaluation transforms experience into insight.

Every time history repeats itself the price goes up. What happens if we repeat our personal history? What happens if we fail to pull some gold from the wreckage of our mistakes? Is it possible to not just survive our greatest mistakes but also have them serve us?

As an author, Teresa boldly, yet humbly, reminds us that life consists more of our personal decisions than from any external conditions. She pulls back the veneer of her life allowing us to connect with her struggles and not just celebrate her successes. Her empathy truly is a superpower so needed in our world today.

Raw. Relatable. Shocking. Vulnerable. Consoling. Provoking.

Each of those words is what I would use to describe the experience of reading this book. As you step into this guided journey, I think you will be forever grateful Teresa chose to say yes to the Holy Spirit and surrender her impressive image for a breathtakingly honest retelling of her story. Thank you, Teresa, for paying the price to offer up this fresh "yes."

Stories have the power to inspire us. True stories have the power to transform us. God is writing a story with your life—a life that is for your good and for His glory. May you hear the tender voice of God as you keep turning the pages of this book.

—Joshua Finley,
speaker, author, coach
joshuafinley.org

Introduction

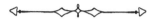

> But when the Father sends the Advocate as my representative—
> that is, the Holy Spirit— he will teach you everything and will
> remind you of everything I have told you.
> John 14:26 (NEW LIVING TRANSLATION)

Why me, you say? But the better question is: why not me? Many of us are eager to accept the good things in life, but rarely the bad. In God's economy, we must be willing to cherish the good gifts (without forgetting the giver of them) and understand that the hard things are also gifts. Do we think we are so special that we should never struggle? We live in a fallen world laden with sin. Free will makes it impossible to live a struggle-free life. We are guaranteed to have struggles; God both blesses and rebukes those He loves. So, why me? Why *not* me. The same situations that apply to the one apply to the other.

The Lord, through the Holy Spirit, is the great communicator and the one who creates understanding. My petition is that *Chasing Easy in a Life of Hard Choices* takes you from "why me?", misunderstanding the reach of God's grace and forgiveness surrounding relationships, unplanned pregnancies, and overall regrettable life decisions, to understanding through the guidance of the Holy Spirit. Amen.

Amid the COVID-19 pandemic, I finally committed to writing. What you are holding in your hands has taken well over forty-two years of life's stuff to happen and the courage to finally put pen to paper. Just as the God of Heaven wrote my story and is still writing it, He is busy writing yours, too. I encourage you to reflect on the past in order to inform your present and to rest in the fact that your future is secure in the One who knows each day before one of them comes to be (Psalm 139:16). Allow that to give you great comfort.

This memoir is my personal journey uncovering some of the most critical decisions I made surrounding life, relationships, pregnancies, and exploring self-discovery. My prayer is that you will treat this memoir with honor and dignity, cherishing the writing on its pages. I will take you from doubt, insecurity, self-loathing, and being dismissive to a life worth living initiated by our Redeemer. It is politically charged, sensitive material. One in three women has had an unplanned pregnancy decision, which begs to say that men have also shared in the experience to varying degrees, but are mostly silent, overlooked, and misunderstood, I believe.

You will walk alongside me, getting an intimate path to the thoughts I had surrounding my choices, the decisions I made, and the battles that ensued with my internal dialogue. Thoughts of inadequacy, insufficiency, and being undeserving of anything other than what I had been handed. These, I discovered later in life, are all lies of the enemy! The book of John reminds us that there is no truth in the devil. "When he lies, he speaks his native language, for he is a liar and the father of lies" (John 8:44b BEREAN STUDY BIBLE). Let's just say I was a prime target

INTRODUCTION

and made his job easy. I needed to decide who I was going to believe: the enemy or my Maker.

Since this book is about choices and the decisions that followed, it is worth noting their definitions. A **decision** is the act of or need for making up one's mind. A **choice** is the right, power, or opportunity to choose. I laid out my options and based my final decisions on what seemed to make the most sense to me with the information I had, however limited it was.

I look back now at what influenced my most critical choices in life, and they were made from a place of fear, ignorance, and pure selfishness.

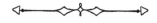

To say I was equipped, well-informed, and mature enough to make some of the decisions I did would be a serious misperception. None of these things happened until my later years. When I was young, I felt that I knew enough to make an educated decision, without seeking the education I needed. Boy, was I way off. Pride prevented me from admitting I didn't have all the answers, so I went with my gut. Not a wise move.

I heard it said in a sermon once, "Information (advice) without experience is just an opinion," therefore I urge you to seek *sound* advice. I've learned when asked for my advice or opinion to preface the response with, "I have never experienced that, but I think....," or "in my own experience, this is what I found..." Reminding myself of this principle helps me to remain authentic.

As we all know, choices are ours to make, but the consequences are predetermined. Some choices will hold favorable outcomes while others may not, but God will use all of it for

His good and perfect plan as He has done for me which I share in this book.

Make good choices. How hard can it be, right? Please don't fret. I did not write this to judge or condemn anyone's decisions. Let's face it, the chances are pretty high that you've made some decisions that you are not proud of, and if you had to do it all over again, you would have made a different choice. I know I surely did. But there is hope!

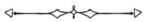

The message is easy—make good choices. Choices that are fully informed, that lead to life, and choices that allow you to live without regrets years down the road.

If you are struggling with decisions surrounding life or death, health or wealth, self-absorption or selflessness, you might find encouragement in these pages, or you might not. I have played on both sides of the fence. I invite you to take the risk and read on. I am of the mindset that the Lord already knew you would be holding this book at precisely this time in your life. Therefore, this book has not landed in your hands by accident.

As someone who was stubborn and refused to believe she needed anyone, I encourage you not to be a lone wolf but instead, surrender your pride and ask for help when and where you need it. Seek God first and He will send you the help you need at precisely the right time. The thought that I had something to say, something of value, something to offer to others, was ridiculous to me. This doubt plagued me, not only years prior to writing this book, but also during the writing process! I wanted to give up countless times. But God saw it through, and you are now holding the labor of love it took to craft my story, God's story.

Introduction

I have already warned you that my story is of a delicate, misunderstood, and controversial nature. Regardless of whether you agree or disagree, you will be exposed to the raw internal dialogue that plagues most women who are faced with an unplanned pregnancy, questionable relationships, and the toxic patterns we cycle in. My journey has affected my immediate family and friends. It is my hope that those who have wrestled with similar decisions about an unplanned pregnancy will find the comfort they seek. May God bless you richly for reading on. *Chasing Easy in a Life of Hard Choices* captures the very essence of who I am and who sustains me today. To the brave hands and hearts that pursue these pages, may your heart be moved to empathy and understanding.

> Therefore encourage one another and build each other up, just as in fact you are doing. —1 Thessalonians 5:11 (NEW INTERNATIONAL VERSION)

In Numbers 22:28 we read, "Then the Lord opened the mouth of the donkey, and she said to Balaam, "What have I done to you, that you have struck me these three times?" Of all places for God to show up.[1] I am not equating Shana to a donkey, but she was God's mouthpiece since the idea that I write my story was first mentioned by Shana, my therapist who specializes in EMDR (Eye Movement Desensitization and Reprocessing) therapy. Yes, I was seeing a therapist, and no, there is no shame in it. God used Shana to plant the seed that birthed the project you are now holding.

Has someone spoken into your life that shared a seemingly absurd God revelation? Can I boldly encourage you to explore the possibility? Because God really does show up in unlikely places. It was my last session with Shana, and I was praying on the way to that session that the Lord would "hit me upside the head with what He wanted me to do." I was discontent, unfulfilled, and yearning for something, but I didn't know what. Have you ever felt that way?

Shana had no idea I was praying this on the drive to see her. When I arrived, the normal greetings and formalities were amiss and instead, she came in with, "You need to write a book to tell your story!" Well, if this wasn't the hit upside the head I prayed for, then I don't know what was. Has the Lord ever answered you so obviously? Secretly I thought, *Oh how cute, but God doesn't want me to write. If he did, He would have told me directly.* And that was my justification for seven years of delayed obedience.

God has a way of showing up when you need that nudge to get going. Shana was my nudge. Look, if the Lord can speak through a donkey, He certainly can speak through a therapist. She went on to justify her declaration. "Out of all the clients I have seen, none have experienced all the options when it comes to pregnancy. You must tell your story for all the others who are scared, uninformed, misinformed, or ill-equipped about their options as a woman with an unplanned pregnancy. Your firsthand knowledge and experience will help countless others."

I was doing the Lord's work in an attempt to ignore the Lord's calling. But you must be brave to share your journey because someone needs to hear it!

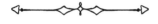

Thank you, Shana, for being bold and for allowing God to speak through you to fulfill His purpose through my story. Again, this was seven years ago. My reason for sharing the time-lapse with you is because I was honestly hoping I could

INTRODUCTION

busy myself with other "ministry activities" and the unsettling in my spirit, which opened the door to discontentment, would go away.

Even though I am not a writer, my peace did not come until—through my obedience to God—I dedicated my attention to writing.

In Hebrews chapter 11 (called the faith chapter), there are ten examples of how faith changed lives. It is my turn to share how faith changed mine. The truth I needed to reconcile is that the Lord always wins! "The mind of man plans his way, but the Lord directs his steps" (Proverbs 16:9 NEW AMERICAN STANDARD BIBLE). So, I decided to get to steppin', and no I don't mean two-steppin' for you country fans, of which I am one. Why forfeit my peace? I have heard it said, if God calls you to it, He will equip you to do it. It was time to put my faith into action.

I recall a book my mom gave me years ago called *The Butterfly Effect* by Andy Andrews.[2] The premise of this book is easy to understand; every decision you make impacts not just yourself but ripples outward to those around you.

Each decision results in an aftermath of either collateral blessings or collateral damage. You choose where that falls once you decide.

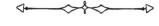

Chasing Easy in a Life of Hard Choices is my recount of the *Butterfly Effect* in action. You will see how the seemingly insignificant and significant decisions surrounding relationships and pregnancies influenced my life and the immediate consequences as well as the lingering effects that are still present today. Some decisions I considered all the options. Others were a knee-jerk reaction and based solely on my personal selfish preference. It was all about me and whether I would be inconvenienced or embarrassed. I never wanted to appear as anything other than having it all together and knowing exactly what I was doing. I was all about my reputation remaining intact. There was no thought into how anyone else might be affected by a decision I was making. It was, after all, my decision.

The test for this truth is pretty simple. Can you still be happy if you don't get your way? If you answer no, then your happiness is directly connected to selfishness. You must get your way to be happy. (Ask me how I know!) Turns out, temper tantrums aren't just for two-year-olds in the middle of the grocery aisle. Adulting is hard. It is a daily task to keep my selfishness in check. I learned over the years that I was the sum of my choices, both good and bad. As Pastor Greg Groeshel of America's largest church put it,

The truth is you cannot be selfish and happy at the same time.

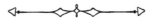

I traded my ultimate for the immediate.

Part 1

Toxic Relationships and the Tragedy of Abortion

Chapter 1

The Egg and the Gift of Manure

> Wait for the Lord; be strong, and let your heart
> take courage, wait for the Lord!
> Psalm 27:14 (ENGLISH STANDARD VERSION)

Have you ever tried to peel a stubborn hard-boiled egg? Surely you have, and I bet you're thinking: "What the heck does this have to do with your book? I thought this was about making choices around an unplanned pregnancy. When do we get to the good stuff?" Hang in there. I promise it will make sense.

Sometimes, I like to eat hard-boiled eggs for my protein snack, but mostly I like them for making deviled eggs. You see, I only knew there was a kitchen in my house because it came with it. I learned to master the art of deviled eggs to contribute to family gatherings, and it was the only thing my family trusted enough from me to eat. I have peeled a lot of eggs. I share this with you because when you peel hard-boiled eggs there are two outcomes: 1) it's super easy and the skin and shell come off in one or two peels and you do the happy dance right there, or 2) you risk pulling off the egg white with the pesky shell that takes forever to peel, bit by measly bit! I have tried several methods to peel eggs smoothly, even buying infomercial gadgets, but they proved to be false advertising! Back to manual labor it was.

Believe me when I tell you, how you deal with the pesky eggshell says a lot about your ability to cope with other subtle, and not so subtle, nuances in life. Do you get frustrated and lose your patience, ultimately throwing the egg away? Or do you remain calm and steady knowing the outcome will be a peeled egg that is less than perfect (with obvious blemishes proving the struggle was real), but you were able to save and use it?

Decisions can be just like peeling hard-boiled eggs!

Hard boiled eggs, when peeling them, are also quite odiferous. My family knows well in advance before reaching the kitchen that I am making deviled eggs. The distinct odor gives it away. The point I'm making is our decisions can stink, too. There are decisions where there doesn't seem to be a right answer, or decisions we made without thinking them through. Sometimes, the toughest decisions will stink simply because they need to be made (funeral arrangements, firing someone, etc.), but the odor will eventually waft away and the air we breathe will be free and clear of the stink.

Unlike the peeled-egg odor that dissipates over time, if we have made decisions we regret, the stink will hang on in the way of bitterness and regret. I know because that's what I did. The roots of bitterness that I left unattended and untreated greatly impacted my ability to cope and ultimately delayed an invitation to heal. Healing can only be done with the help and guidance of the Lord Jesus Christ through His Spirit.

I had an abortion at fifteen. I kept the turmoil that stirred below the surface hidden. I thought I was over it. It didn't affect me one way or the other. I learned the hard way that one seemingly harmless decision had indeed impacted me in ways I would discover thirty-five years later. I truly felt like a modern-day Israelite, only the wandering was in the wilderness of my mind. I believed I had the right to hang onto bitterness and regret which prolonged my recovery. Would there be a promised land for me? If I would have known or had access to counseling about the aftermath of abortion and its influence on my life, I could have spared myself all those years of wandering. My ignorance and denial led to over a quarter of a century of choices I would later regret.

> Where there is no guidance, a people falls, but in an abundance of counselors there is safety. — Proverbs 11:14 (ESV)

It is estimated that the average adult makes 65,000 decisions a day. Some are ostensibly easy, peaceful, and rewarding almost as if someone guided the decision, and others are ones that you make out of sheer need and they nag at you until you pull the trigger on the final decision. Some decisions stink, and others flourish.

Just like that pesky shell, we make small decisions on the way to big ones. When things don't go your way, if you err on the side of frustration as opposed to calm endurance, you'll end up with skinned knees. Take it from me: invite wise, godly counsel into your life. You still get to choose but having multiple perspectives will help equip your decisions and be a positive influence on your final answers. Here's to tolerating peskiness, stench, insecurities, and forging on despite them.

> Rejoice always, pray without ceasing, **give thanks in all circumstances**; for this is the will of God in Christ Jesus for you. —1 Thessalonians 5:16–18 (ESV; emphasis mine)

There was a little boy who always saw the good in every situation. His envious older brother asked his parents to test his little brother's optimism. He suggested that for Christmas his parents wrap a box of manure as a gift. Reluctantly his parents agreed. They wondered how anyone, even little Tommy, could find something positive from a box of manure. Both boys were raised the same way: to expect good things even if they didn't look good at the moment, to remain full of hope and wonder, and to trust their mom and dad to know what was best for them. This laid the foundation for Tommy's reaction. I find it interesting that the boys were raised by the same set of parents with the same upbringing and had opposite dispositions. One was the glass half-empty kind of kid, and one was the glass half-full kind.

Christmas day came and little Tommy opened the "test" box. He was so excited and immediately ran out of the house into the yard. Not finding what he was looking for outside, he thought, "it must be inside!" He came charging back into the house checking all the rooms and finally, out of breath, stopped in the middle of the living room. His parents asked why he was so excited about opening a box of manure. Little Tommy declared with zeal, "With this special gift, I know there must be a pony somewhere!"

> If you then, who are evil, know how to give good gifts to your children, how much more

will your Father who is in heaven give good things to those who ask him! —Matthew 7:11

May this parable[3] resonate with you as you go through life's stuff. We, too, are shaped by our perception and interpretation which results in our attitude and ultimate reaction. My childhood lens was rosy. However, that rosiness changed to a clouded lens after several heartbreaking instances that challenged my belief in myself and the goodness of people.

My definition of the "mom" role was to guide, protect, and sometimes challenge your children for their own good. To allow them to flirt with disappointment, to make mistakes, to make their own (age-appropriate) decisions, and to discover more about themselves through living. With my mom, I often felt attacked as opposed to mentored and the result was a strained relationship. It is an important note because, you see, I didn't give my mom the benefit of the doubt. We butted heads most of my adult life. I thought she didn't know anything. Turns out she knew most everything. It was only after her sudden death in October of 2017 that I realized just how much *I misunderstood her*. (I love you and miss you every day, Mom!) She inspired *Chasing Easy in a Life of Hard Choices*. Her life was filled with hard choices based on a childhood of abuse and neglect. She wanted to help make life easier for her children in hopes to spare us from disaster. However, she also knew when to stand down and allow us to learn.

Me, Mom and Kimmie 2008

Who do you misunderstand, or are you the one that's misunderstood? Everything we do, say, and create communicates to those around us. Is our meaning and motivation always solid and clear to those we are communicating to or with? Doubtful. Why doubtful? We are all programmed by our surroundings, our experiences, our trials, our hurts, our failures, our victories, and the people in our lives (permanently, by happenstance, or by selection). We have developed an understanding of life based on this criterion. This is what has shaped us, and this is what colors our perception of life. Did you ever stop to think that everything we know we have learned from someone else?

Our perception and what we choose to believe about a situation forms our truth, which ultimately determines our response and the outcome.

The next time you are involved in a conversation, take notice of how many times you offer advice, and whether you agree or disagree on the subject matter. One person can say the sky is blue and you think it's red (not because you're colorblind, either). Have you seen the "Gold Dress Challenge" asking what color you see, gold or blue?[4] This brilliantly challenges our perception of the way we see life's stuff through our lens. I bring the dress challenge into the picture because it relates to how we see life. When we look at someone else's life, be it good or bad, we have no idea what it took them to get where they are. Either we are envious of their riches, popularity, or ease in life, or we are scowling at the indignance of an offender. *How could they?* The truth is, both circumstances could have come from the same background. In any given situation, do we offer grace and mercy, or are we quick to judge and condemn?

I have been inspired by two quotes from Elizabeth Gilbert's book, *Big Magic*.[5] The first one is, "Whether you are young or old, we need your work in order to enrich and inform our own lives," and my favorite, **"You already know so much more than you think you know. You are not finished; you are merely ready."** Here's to being ready.

The motivation to write, other than obedience to God's prompting, came from the sincere desire to help someone else in similar circumstances with the intention of living out my life verse, "Praise be to the God and Father of our Lord Jesus Christ, the Father of compassion and the God of **all** comfort, who comforts us in **all** our troubles, so that we can comfort those in any trouble with the comfort we ourselves receive from God. For just as we share abundantly in the sufferings of Christ, so also our comfort abounds through Christ!" (2 Corinthians 1:3–5 NIV; emphasis mine).

My pastor, Josh Finley, reminded me that "Someone is waiting on the other side of your obedience and if your why is strong enough, the how will be tolerable." Words of wisdom on both counts. If your *why* (the motivation and inspiration behind what you do) isn't strong enough you will abandon the *how* (accomplishing God's will through His provisions), which I did for seven years. I knew I was chosen to experience what I did for the benefit of others, but I didn't believe my life experience was significant enough to put into words. I was secretly hoping that someone else would write it so I wouldn't have to. The Lord, however, always wins. If your why is strong enough, it will be like the dross of silver being refined by heat (trials) until the beauty of the final product is revealed. That, my friend, is rewarding. I have had to reflect on my why more than once to continue with this project and see it to completion. Circling back to the gift of manure:

It is in the trials, wrong choices, and the consequences I suffered that led to seeing the "manure" of life as steppingstones and opportunities for growth.

I surely did not see the beauty in life's stuff in the moment. God always has a plan. As I near sixty years old, I would say I am now mature in manure. Joyce Meyer said once on stage, "There is no drive-through breakthrough. You must 'go through' in order to grow."

Consider me grown.

Chapter 2

You Always Remember Your First

Everything is permissible for me—but not everything is beneficial.
1 Corinthians 6:12a (NIV)

Flee from sexual immorality. All other sins a man commits are outside his body, but he who sins sexually sins against his own body. Do you not know that your body is a temple of the Holy Spirit, who is in you, whom you have received from God? You are not your own; you were bought at a price. Therefore, honor God with your body.
1 Cor 6:18–20

To be completely transparent, since I sometimes have a hard time remembering my kids' names, I might not get every detail of my teen years correct. What I will get correct are the emotions surrounding the choices I made and the resulting consequences at the innocent, naïve, and tender age of fifteen.

I was the athletic type in high school and received the most attention and praise when I did well in gymnastics, softball, soccer, and basically anything that involved a ball. This is when

I learned the art of acceptance through performance. (For those of you familiar with personality types, I am an Enneagram 3, the Successful Achiever.) I have a hard time "feeling" and tapping into my emotions. I do better planning, strategizing, and accomplishing a goal than I do acknowledging my emotions.

These were the days when high school began in the tenth grade. You already "survived" the awkward middle grades, seventh through ninth, and prayed you would stay friends over the summer with your core group so entering high school wouldn't be so bad. There were three groups of students, and depending on which group you identified with, determined your lot in school.

Everyone wants to fit in, belong, and be accepted. It is how we are wired by our Maker. Whether you are an adolescent or an adult, we all have this innate desire to be accepted and loved. Each group had their own identification and different levels of popularity. There were the popular "jocks" (a term that covered both the girl and boy athletes), the "nerds" (the smart geeks, popular within their own setting) and the least popular "heads" (the explorative druggie types).

The jocks (my group) had an air of superiority and seemed to be the most exclusive. The heads explored the next high, and the nerds sat on the student council, debate committee, yearbook committee, and were the class representatives trying to keep the rest of us in line, which was a tall order. The jocks had big egos, the heads had a "Cheech and Chong" swagger, and the nerds were the teacher's pet.

The jocks, being the most popular, were able to recruit others to do their dirty work such as writing their papers or giving them their study notes before exams. The nerds were usually up for hire by the jocks, so, in that regard they gained some popularity by association, and the heads were the ones cutting class to get high and usually barely got by enough to graduate. If you wanted to learn how to cut class on Senior Hook Day, you learned from the heads.

Now, these are generalizations. There were heads who excelled, not just in extracurricular drug use, but in school academics. Case in point, I remember one girl who never studied, wasn't shy about getting high, and she was a straight-A student! There were jocks who befriended heads and nerds who befriended jocks. So, there was some cross-pollination of sorts between the groups.

As a jock, I played all things sports. Softball was my jam, then came gymnastics, and last came soccer. It is odd that I played soccer because I despise running today, but I did come across some high school pictures as proof. Unlike other fifteen-year-old jocks, I was a sensitive spirit and didn't like leaving anyone out. Before you think I was a saint, I am positively certain there were times that I played along with ridicule to stay popular and left others out. But I have conveniently erased that from my memory. This was a coping mechanism I would learn later in life and how I dealt with most unpleasant memories. Isn't that what we do to protect ourselves? We bury those unwanted memories never to be recalled again. Until they are!

I had friends from all groups, the nerds, the heads, and the jocks. I wanted to learn through experience but was careful not to lose my footing and popularity by engaging too much with the other groups. I knew then what I declare now:

I was moving along just fine in the 10th grade, doing okay in school, and excelling in sports. I was on top of the world. I had been working at Burger King for two years to have extra cash for the things I wanted to do because if I wanted something, I was taught early on to work for it. There were very few of us in that generation that lived in luxury or felt entitled to everything. Nothing was handed to me, except the concept of working hard for what you wanted. I rode my bike to and from work and made a little over two dollars an hour. I had zero interest in boys, unless it was to play football, baseball, dodgeball, build tree forts, build ramps to jump ravines and ditches, or go dirt-bike riding. I was every bit a tomboy. I preferred the company of boys because there was hardly any backstabbing, gossiping, and other drama like there was with girls. Boys were not my thing, until they were, or should I say, *until he was.*

The grapevine, a.k.a. the rumor mill, revealed that Mike, the most popular senior in school, had his eye on me. This was both flattering and puzzling to me at the same time. I was not developed like most of the other girls, which I blame on sports and genetics. I also was not the flirtatious, hey-look-at-me type. I was tough, which was safe and kept boys at a distance. My immediate reaction to this rumor was that it was a joke or a bet he didn't want to lose. I didn't know why he would be interested in me. This is where the new sensation of comparison and the insecurity that followed began to seep in. I was very confident when it came to sports, but this boy's interest in me was a new thing. I didn't like it, but I didn't know how to combat it either. Theodore Roosevelt once said that "comparison is the thief of joy,"[6] and I wholeheartedly agree.

Misunderstanding stems from ignorance. To understand, you must seek to know. Without knowledge, what you think you know will be inconclusive and unsupported.

A short time after this rumor had circulated, lo and behold, Mike asked me out. Back then, we called it hooking up, but today that phrase has a much different meaning which I learned from my teenage girls. The first time I asked my daughter who she was hooking up with, her face was aghast, and she said, "Mom, we aren't hooking up!" I had no idea what the big deal was until they both explained what it meant in today's culture. Yikes! I have not used this term since that gentle correction. If you don't know, ask a teenager.

Mike and I started dating and I realized I liked the attention. The attention from him was special and the extra attention I got from other students was a bonus. It was very different from prior exposure where I saw boys as mere competition for a position in sports. This was different. The way he looked at me, almost as if looking into my soul, the way he spoiled me with surprises and gifts, and the manner in which he talked me up in front of his friends. He was proud of me. He was a gentleman, too. I also liked how he included me in guy stuff like rebuilding the engine on a Pontiac Tempest. Okay, full disclosure: I simply held some bolts to attach the engine to the firewall, but I felt invigorated, important, and as if I could conquer anything with him. I mattered. What was especially rewarding was when he would choose me over his friends, doing something he probably didn't want to do, but did because he cared about my happiness.

There wasn't a class in school called "How to Prevent Feelings of Insecurity" or I would have signed up for it as an elective.

I was falling in love, or what I thought was love. Today I would describe this "love" as counterfeit. But at fifteen, I knew all there was to know about love. Didn't you? How do you process these new and gooey feelings if not to share with your brood (or in today's language tribe)? Surely the other girls I hung out with were familiar with what I was feeling, after all, I was the last to date in our group. So, I sought their "wise council" on what to do to be a good girlfriend. They said things like make yourself available, follow through with what might be uncomfortable (closeness, intimacy), pretend to like to do something even if you don't, etc. Their counsel was vague. I wish they had just said, "you are expected to have sex." I didn't turn to my parents for advice because they weren't exactly role models for love. Let's just say they did the best they could after being married at age sixteen and nineteen. Shoot, they were kids themselves but managed to stay married for fifty-four years!

Anyway, about a year into our dating he told me he loved me. Yes! Isn't that what every girl wants to hear? With this proclamation, I just knew how I wanted my future to unfold. We were going to get married, buy the house with a white picket fence, have children, and live happily ever after. Or so I thought. Then *it* happened. As a child, my choices forced me to make grown-up decisions.

Mike was a senior and I was a sophomore. The coveted Senior Prom was fast approaching, and I felt secure in knowing I was going to be going with the most popular boy in school. I didn't have to vie for the attention of who I wanted an invitation from nor did I have to compete for the position. In the early eighties, it wasn't cool to go with a bunch of girlfriends like it is today, shunning the need to compete or feeling inferior because you weren't asked to prom. But whether it's "cool" or not, there is always a choice. Some choices will affect you for the rest of your life.

Two months from prom night I realized I had missed my period. I wasn't really concerned because I had heard *you can't get pregnant the first time you have sex*. Plus, I was so physically active that sometimes I missed a period here and there because of the athletic stress I put my body through. Then I started to feel funny. Now I was worried, so I took a pregnancy test which revealed that I was pregnant. I tried to convince myself that the test was wrong, that it was a false positive. To be sure, I took a few more and they all returned positive. I was in complete denial, even angry at the possibility. I was at a loss. I had no idea what to do. I was confused. I was hurt. I was tormented. I was scared. I needed help. I needed guidance. I couldn't tell anyone. I couldn't tell my sister; she was too young. I couldn't tell my parents; they'd disown me.

I had to tell my boyfriend. How do you gracefully deliver such news? Oh, how I wrestled with the consequence of what I allowed to happen. It was my fault. Why didn't I say no? What was I trying to prove? I was under a huge cloud of regret, disappointment in myself, and feeling dirty, although I didn't really understand why. Leading up to this pivotal discovery, Mike and I were having the time of our lives and really enjoying each other's company. Delivering this news was going to threaten everything. Much to my surprise, Mike didn't seem shocked. I secretly questioned if this had happened to him before. I quickly shut that thought down so as not to add to the crazy thoughts I already had. One crisis at a time. I really thought I was going crazy. I was relying on Mike to tell me what to do, but he didn't know what to do either. I was fifteen, scared, confused, and hoping for an answer that didn't include telling my parents. I was overwhelmed.

We decided to consult Mike's older sister. It turned out that she would have *the* answer. She asked around and heard about this procedure—abortion—that would help you take care of the unwanted "blob of tissue." She provided us the help and guidance we needed. *It's not a baby* echoed in my head. *It's best for everyone* I thought which gave me peace of mind. I thought it would be harmless. My rationale was that it would save everyone the embarrassment of having a baby "out of wedlock" and afterwards, we could simply carry on with our lives and our relationship would not be inconvenienced by a baby. Of course, we would continue as normal without interruption, right? Especially since Mike loved me. I was dead wrong.

Breaking down the thoughts that went into my decision were trifold: 1) how can I possibly have a baby that I can't support? 2) I am still in high school; it would ruin my future and my life, but more importantly, 3) I can't disappoint my parents and friends. What would people think? Other than the thought that my life was over, if I had the baby, what other people thought was most important to me. I didn't want to tarnish the good-girl reputation I had. I was paralyzed by fear. *If I take care of it now, it's not a baby, and so there is no harm. No one must know. It will only hurt me.* I kept rationalizing and justifying my decision to abort. I was ignorant. I was immature. I was a child. I was misinformed and I misunderstood the consequences that would follow for decades, consequences that shaped my perception of life creating a wounded and tormented soul. I wanted to numb the reality of what I was considering. My wall of denial protected me from confronting the emotional trauma, but it also prevented forgiveness and love from breaking in.

In all my internal dialogue, the most important factor was amiss. I did not consider the "blob of tissue" as a child growing in my womb who had a heartbeat (this occurs at day 21) when I made the decision to abort. I didn't know, and I honestly, subconsciously, didn't want to find out anything contrary to my misinformed belief of what was inside me. Sheer ignorance and fear held me prisoner in my own mind. What I was about to sign up for came down to a choice, but how does a child at fifteen make a life-or-death choice about the child they are carrying?

I needed support in a way that I would not have understood. I needed someone I trusted enough not to gossip and to lay out all the facts of my options—parenting, adoption, and abortion—before I would make a final decision. Sadly, there was no such person in my life. The girls I did know only knew of two options, parenting, and abortion. Or better known as life and death.

Here's the thing about choices. You can choose to do whatever you want, but you cannot choose the consequence. You must be willing to accept whatever the consequences are that your choice dictates and often, there are consequences that you never consider when you make your decision. I know that's what I did. Mike and I never considered parenting. The only option we discussed was abortion. Adoption, as a life choice, never entered the picture. Sadly, in today's society, abortion is still favored over adoption. *What?* While my abortion experience was forty-two years ago, the public perception has not changed.

My boyfriend said he could pay for the procedure and would take me to the appointment and that this was the only option that was best for everyone (everyone except the "blob of tissue"). We were ignorant of what the advice of his older sister would mean for us and the life inside me, but we heeded it anyway. In her defense, she had no idea that what she was suggesting would change my life and his life forever. There were no resources readily available to educate myself on my options. There was no one holding my hand to comfort me and inform me that there were three options when faced with an unplanned pregnancy—parenting, adoption, and abortion. There wasn't a hotline that I could call to discuss my situation. If there was a crisis pregnancy center that offered family counseling, I was not aware of it. I felt alone, isolated, and defeated. I personally was too ashamed and too embarrassed to ask anyone for advice. Even if the resources of a crisis pregnancy center and educational resources existed back then, I believe the guilt I carried over the pregnancy would have been stronger than the morally right thing to do. Since I was already thinking abortion was the best option, I was easily convinced by Mike to follow through with it. I scheduled the abortion.

I think it's important to recognize that when I called to make the appointment, the woman on the other end of the phone was very patient, sweet, compassionate, and understanding. She made me feel accepted and not judged. I felt a sense of relief after talking to her. How ironic. I remember Mike taking one of his best friends with us to the appointment. I was confused and wondered why he went with us. I was too self-absorbed at this point to think that maybe Mike needed support, too. The reason we were able to "take care of it" was because Mike worked and was able to come up with the money to afford the procedure.

When we showed up to the clinic, Mike and his friend sat down while I checked in. It wasn't until I turned around that I realized there were no empty seats in the waiting room. Let me remind you that this was over forty years ago. I had to sit on my boyfriend's lap to have a seat. The waiting room itself was full of other singles and couples who were there for the same reason. The room was cold and dark. The windows, which lined one wall, were covered with dark shades, keeping the identity of those inside protected. There were no smiles and the posture was one of shame and guilt with heads hung low. We all just sat there nervously waiting for our names to be called and escorted back to the procedure room.

I remember my palms were sweaty. I was more nervous that the procedure would hurt me than for the fact that I was choosing to end an innocent life—something I didn't yet believe.

I had no idea what an abortion entailed. We didn't have the internet back then to research and look up how the procedure was performed. I was not aware of a crisis pregnancy center offering education and hope. There was nowhere to go for a free sonogram to make sure the pregnancy was viable. Again, the resources available today were nonexistent. My ignorance about the procedure, about the fact that the fetus was a person, and that my decision would have consequences that would take me through the rest of my life, overshadowed my judgment. Leading up to the procedure, I was too embarrassed to tell anyone what was going on, but when my boyfriend leaked the news, there were other girls that came forward that reassured me that it was no big deal, that having an abortion was all part of growing up, and that "everyone does it." It was almost like a rite of passage. But abortion is not birth control!

I wanted to get this over with and move on with my life like it never happened. I wanted immediate relief, but that didn't happen. When my name was called, the nurse escorted me to the room. I felt like I was being led by a noose. I didn't want to follow through with this. Deep down I knew it was wrong. I just kept repeating in my head, *This is what you need to do to carry on without interruptions to your life and plans. Mike paid for it and now you must follow through with your end of the deal.* Once again, I didn't want to disappoint anyone.

When we arrived at the room, I noticed how cold it was. I was so scared. There were no pictures on the walls, not even the scrubs the nurse wore had any fun print on them. The walls were as blank as the stares from the staff. This was not a typical doctor's visit. There was nothing warm about the room or the doctor, I would find out. I was directed to strip, put on the hospital gown, and sit on the cold metal table until the doctor was ready. There was a distinct odor that I couldn't quite put my finger on. I know the doctor was busy because of all those patients I saw in the waiting room. I remember asking the nurse if it was going to hurt and she said I might feel some cramping, but that I would be fine. I wasn't fine. (And it hurt a whole lot more than my worst cramps ever did!) I wondered if the nurse ever had an abortion herself to make such a claim.

I remember the loud suction noise and I remembered, after the procedure, looking at the remnants of what had just happened. I did not know what I was looking at. I also didn't know that they had to account for all the parts of the baby. I learned from my brother-in-law the medical term for this accounting is called Products of Conception (POC). But in the movie *Unplanned* (2019),[7] based on the memoir of the same title by Abby Johnson, they give a more fitting name for this term, "Parts of Children." This practice of POC is to make sure the abortion was complete, otherwise there is a greater risk for infection if not all parts are accounted for. The problem is there is no one policing the business of abortion. The risks of abortion are further complicated by the lack of accountability for operating a clean and safe facility. Abortion clinics are not held to the same standards as hospitals, as seen in the movie *Gosnell*,[8] even though they are performing surgical procedures.

If you do your own research, you will realize that you are being fed a lie that abortion is perfectly safe. The clinics won't tell you directly about botched abortions, deaths caused by the procedure, the emotional trauma, or the failed abortion attempts where babies are born alive. In this instance, the nurse has two options: leave the room until the baby stops breathing on its own or rescue the baby. You will not hear of the women who lost their lives because of a botched abortion nor will you hear the information about the women who are rushed off to an emergency room because the abortionist and the clinic are not equipped to handle emergencies. Take every precaution to understand fully what you are about to walk into. Educate yourself, inform your decision, and then decide. Be aware of the risks and complications—this is surgery, after all. Ask questions and learn what type of abortion will be performed.[9]

Please understand: what I thought was a temporary fix for a temporary "inconvenience" haunted me for years and years. It wasn't until I was introduced to a Bible study for post-abortive women called *Forgiven and Set Free* by Linda Cochrane[10] that I found healing. It was a difficult journey, for sure. Another great book for self-paced study is *Her Choice to Heal* by Sydna Masse.[11] If this is the first time you are hearing of a healing or recovery journey from abortion, be brave and take the chance.

I naively thought with the abortion behind us, Mike and I could go on with life as usual. I thought it would be that easy. Again, I was fifteen and trusted my older, wiser boyfriend. What I didn't realize was that my high school sweetheart, who was my first love, was constantly running around with other girls. I was too naïve to understand what was going on. When I finally faced the truth, I was devastated. I couldn't understand how he could tell me he loved me only to repeat those sacred words to several other girls. I no longer trusted in "love" or my perception of love. However, I was not ready to give up or walk away and begged Mike not to leave me.

We stayed together another three years until I overheard him say to his friend, "I don't love Teresa" and laughed like I was nothing. *Our relationship meant NOTHING?* I couldn't breathe. My heart was racing, my palms sweating. I felt like the whole

This is what I got in return for giving away the most sacred part of my being.

world was crashing down on me. My knees went weak. *Surely, he didn't mean that. I was a "good" girlfriend. He was joking, right?* Even so, it would be a sick joke. I gave myself away for "the love of my life" and was under the impression he felt the same way. I felt destroyed, humiliated, embarrassed, rejected, and abandoned. I felt unworthy, worthless, like damaged goods.

How was I going to go on without him? Maybe I could forgive and forget? I was convinced that I would never find anyone better than Mike, or anyone to treat me as good as he did. *Yeah sure, he had a few flings, but he always came back to me, so I still win. Right?* What kind of crazy talk was this? I was faithful. He wasn't. I was willing to sacrifice myself to turn the other (embarrassed) cheek. I wanted to prove a few of my girlfriends wrong who warned me about his charade that it would be different with me. He wouldn't run around on me. I could be the best girlfriend ever and he would change. I was so naïve. I should have heeded the obvious warning signs, but it was easier for me to go on knowing I had a boyfriend, flaws and all, than to not be loved by someone regardless of how tainted that love was. He managed to keep his extracurricular affairs hidden well for a long time. Or did I choose to ignore the signs for a long time? However, the Bible warns that what is done in secret will come to the light (Luke 12:2–3). Let's just say he was lit up.

This was the first of many failed relationships and the debilitating, negative self-image that followed. What I found that contributed greatly to my healing was post-abortive care. I had no idea what it was, what it entailed, or that it even existed. In the book of Isaiah, we are promised a double portion for our shame (Isaiah 61:7)!

Abortion carries a weight all its own and shame and disgrace for me were ever-present without me knowing it. Please consider post-abortive care if you or someone you know needs healing from a past abortion. Take it from me: it is life changing. And God will use you in ways you never knew, all for His glory.

Senior Prom ,as a Sophomore , with Mr. Andover.

Chapter 3

The Barbarism of Late-Term Abortion

> Now we see things imperfectly, like puzzling reflections in a mirror, but then we will see everything with perfect clarity. All that I know now is partial and incomplete, but then I will know everything completely, just as God now knows me completely.
> 1 Corinthians 13:12 (NLT)

> Consider it pure joy, my brothers and sisters, whenever you face trials of many kinds, because you know that the testing of your faith produces perseverance. Let perseverance finish its work so that you may be mature and complete, not lacking anything.
> James 1:2–4 (NIV)

If you are thinking that a woman who discovers she is pregnant acts on her own (yes, some do), I'd like to share a few scenarios with you to broaden your mind. This first account about late-term abortion may be hard to hear, but it needs to be told. In January 2019, New York became the sixth state that approves abortions up to the ninth month. This clearly is no longer a "blob of tissue," but a fully formed baby with prominent features. The state approval of late-term abortion hit close to home. My twins, who are now twenty-one years old, were born at seven months weighing 2 lb. 10 oz. and 2 lb. 12 oz. They were born premature; however, they are thriving today. They were both raised with the same respect for life when considering options from an unintended pregnancy. Interestingly, one daughter is pro-life and the other pro-choice.

Here is my question: What right does the preborn have to life? We are told by society to protect those that have no voice. Do you think that includes children in the womb? As a woman, who at fifteen had an abortion, I promise you I am not being self-righteous here. I messed up. I have repented, and I am forgiven. The same will be extended to you through grace. Another question I have is this: will the "personhood" amendment ever be passed?[12] Why do we choose to discredit life beginning at conception as the Physicians' Desk Reference (PDR)[13] would teach? *How can we possibly think late-term abortion is okay?*

Did you know that if a pregnant woman is involved in a no-fault car accident and someone hits her and the unborn child dies as a result, it is considered manslaughter? Where is the rationale then? Time to get real. To hear a hard truth. Remember, I warned you that this story may be hard to hear, but as opposed to covering up the ugly truth, I am exposing it for your consideration. Christian singer Matthew West reminds of this when he sings, "Truth be told, the truth is rarely told."[14]

Samantha's Story

In the summer of her eighth-grade year, at age 13, she lost her virginity.

"It was the 'cool thing' to do. And you can't get pregnant the first time. Besides, everyone else was doing it... so, why not?"

A few months into the school year, she started to feel nauseous and was tired all the time. She convinced herself it was her body getting older and changing. She was in high school now. That must be it. By January, her mom sent her to the doctor to see what was wrong. The doctor informed her after the exam that she was pregnant. She was stunned and in disbelief.

"The only time I did anything was five months ago. That can't be it! Plus, you can't get pregnant the first time anyway!"

After the family doctor called her parents in, they had to decide what to do—quickly. This was a late-term pregnancy and according to her parents, abortion was the *only* option. She asked questions but, in the end, her parents and the doctor convinced her that she had no other option. There's no way her parents were going to allow her, a freshman in high school, to keep the baby. Her mother told her in order to spare the "family reputation," she was not to have the baby.

(Maybe this scenario is familiar to you. Maybe you, like Samantha, were convinced by the people you loved and trusted the most. Or maybe you had nowhere to turn for sound advice on all your options, and therefore acted alone. Whatever your reason, God can redeem you!)

The doctor recommended the best late-term abortion clinic; however, it was halfway across the country. So off they flew to a Kansas clinic that specialized in late-term abortions. The procedure would take five days. Samantha would soon find that there was no shortage of girls seeking the same relief. There were ten other girls in the waiting room. *Did their parents and their doctors convince them to be here, like mine did?* she thought. *Were they alone in this, were they forced to abort a 25-week or older baby? Who would support them once it was over? Where were the fathers of the babies in all of this?* She knew in her head and her heart this was wrong.

"I knew it was wrong—every step of the way. But I didn't have any help."

The first four days her cervix was unnaturally expanded, repeatedly, in order that the baby would pass through the birth canal. After every treatment, she would go back to the hotel in severe pain, curl up in a ball, and cry. *Why am I doing this?* Toward the end of the agonizing week-long procedure, she was on the procedure table and felt the baby kicking. She'd felt the baby move before but figured it was indigestion. But not this time.

"It dawned on me; this is the baby kicking me! I'm talking about crazy moves, like somersaults! It was actually hurting me!"

The doctor entered the room holding a long needle, and told her, "This will all be over soon." Panic set in. She imagined the baby was kicking so hard because it sensed the reality of what was about to happen. With the baby kicking more vigorously and her crying, the doctor inserted the long needle into her abdomen and almost immediately, the baby stopped kicking. She never felt the baby move again. (In case you are curious, the solution in the needle stopped the baby's heartbeat which began beating on day 21.)

"So now I have murdered my child, and I have to carry her around inside me."

She felt her spirit die. She hated herself and everyone around her. She had to go back to the clinic one last time to "finish the process." She was put in a large room of girls where their beds formed a circle around the nurse's station. She was numb. She, like everyone else, had an IV in her arm that fed her medicine making her groggy and listless. She assumed this was to help them forget what had happened. It didn't work. You can't forget something like that. She would remember every gruesome detail. Everything.

The nurse stopped at each bed and checked the girls for dilation. One by one, the girls were wheeled out to another room. As she laid there shivering, she realized that not one of the pro-abortion people had yet to comfort or coach any of the girls, not one, although this is what was promised when the appointment was set. Not one staff member stopped by her bed to show sympathy or support. If they wanted you to think they were there for you, why didn't anyone talk to them? Where was the compassion? They were as cold as the procedure table. They just left us there on our beds cold, shaking, and scared. She felt invisible.

"At one point I was shaking so badly, a nurse walked by and tossed a blanket on the bed and kept on walking; she didn't even look at me!"

The nurse came over to her bedside, shoved her hand under the blanket and decided that she was dilated enough. It was her turn. She got in the wheelchair, IV and all. They wheeled her to a room that resembled a janitor's broom closet, but with a toilet. The nurse helped her shaking body out of the chair, placed her on the toilet seat and said, "Push." So, she did.

"I have no idea what happened to my child, but that's where I left her—in a toilet! What was wrong with me?"

They wheeled her to yet another room after that to continue to "finish the process." The nurse who wheeled her there put a hand on her belly and said, "Look how skinny you are now!" As if *that* was her first priority. As if that was something she even cared about. All she could think about was she just did the worst thing in the world.

"Not only did I kill something, but I killed my own child, and I hated myself for it."

Once home, she lost her will to live. She hated herself, her parents, and every woman passing by with a baby stroller. She hated life and wanted to die. Literally. She purposely chose to be self-destructive by turning to drugs, looking to numb the pain, and eventually hoped to overdose. She ran wild with other teenagers who offered danger. She hoped to be in a guy's car when he took a corner too fast, hoping he'd flip the car. Her parents realized the magnitude of her behavior and got her into therapy. Therapy? The very people that took her to end her daughter's life, now wanted to save hers? Ironic. After multiple diagnoses and even more prescriptions, no therapy or medication worked. She still wanted to die.

Fast forward ten years later. She finally found a therapist she liked, who decided that she was suffering from Post-Traumatic Stress Disorder, PTSD, from the abortion. The medical field now recognizes this as Post Abortive Stress Syndrome, PASS.[15] The therapist recommended a retreat designed for women in the same situation. She reluctantly agreed. Her therapist not only got her registered but paid for the event. (See how God was working here?) It changed her life. She met other woman who had gone through the same experience. They built a comradery. They made life-long friends. They healed, together.

"I felt an overwhelming forgiveness from God; He still loved me!"

After everything she had done and everything she had been through, she realized that weekend that God would take her back, no matter what. When she took this wisdom home with her, she stopped hanging out with bad crowds, stopped doing drugs, and gave herself some much-needed forgiveness. She started attending church again and eventually met her husband and had two precious daughters. But if you think she galloped into the sunset and lived happily ever after...not quite.

"I'm still a wreck. Sometimes I have to pull off to the side of the road and cry. I have flashbacks of the horror of not giving the first baby a chance."

Even after all these years, she has constant reminders. Yet she considers herself one of the few women who found healing. She knows there are thousands of others who haven't found healing and are still hurting. She begs those who are at a crossroad to:

"Take whatever God is putting in your heart and put an end to abortion —we have to, because we can."

Samantha's story is a powerful reminder of the influence our mothers have on us. Maybe it wasn't your mother, but a boyfriend, a husband, a friend, a counselor, social media, or an acquaintance that influenced you. Be careful who you listen to. If what they say doesn't line up with Scripture, run as far away as you can as quickly as you can. Seek God.

In my research, I wondered how lost fatherhood affected the baby's father? What was their perspective? I chose the word "father" because anyone can father a child. It takes a special man to be a daddy.

I want to share with you the testimony of Greg Smalley, a preacher and author, who recalls the moment he took his college girlfriend to a women's care center for a sonogram. Innocently enough, they walked into this "women's care center" that was camouflaged as an abortion facility. I imagine no one would get caught walking into a neon-signed building with "Abortions Performed Here" flashing over the door, as opposed to a women's care center. (But this is the clever hook they use to get unsuspecting women to walk in the door. I ran into a young woman once from Planned Parenthood who set up a display table at the B'More Healthy Expo.[16] These people are trained to say they are interested in the best health choices for women; however, in the next breath she shared that there are "abortion scholarships" available for women who want one and can't afford the "health care" they need.)

The nurse confirmed the pregnancy was viable and then proceeded to say, "we can take care of this today." And that's what they did. A spontaneous, innocent gesture turned horribly wrong by the suggestion of a stranger. He now reflects on his missed opportunity at fatherhood and is often moved to tears. He regrets not giving their little boy a chance. Why didn't they walk out of the clinic? What made him think it was okay to stay? He missed an opportunity to choose life and it haunts him to this day.

In another heartbreaking testimony, a man in his sixties talks about how he convinced his girlfriend to have an abortion. Over forty years later and married to this same girl for most of the forty years, it still haunts them both. Lastly, another man whose wife, unbeknownst to him, had two abortions before they had their two later children. He questioned himself and questioned why his wife didn't trust him enough to share that she was pregnant and what she was considering. Instead, she took it upon herself without consulting him and decided they were not ready for children. **Could he have changed her heart and mind to spare his earlier children? He will never know.**

What must be going through the mind of a man who is made aware of an unplanned pregnancy? Where does he go for wisdom or guidance? What is he thinking when he finds out after an abortion has taken place? Pregnancy is the worst fear most have when engaging in sex (protected or not), instead of the fact that they are more likely to contract a disease, as statistics would show. There are over thirty sexually transmitted diseases today, up from five in the 1980s.[17] When you sleep with someone, you need to realize you are sleeping with everyone they've ever slept with. Crazy, right? There is wisdom that surpasses understanding when you save the best gift of intimacy for your future spouse. **Virginity is not a dirty word!**

praying for the lives lost in a former abortion procedure room.

I didn't think my research would be complete without enlisting the help of some male friends. I reached out to my friend, Mike Martelli, and he suggested I talk to Dennis for additional insight. For five years, this man counseled the fathers of preborn babies while the mothers were being counseled in a private room at the pregnancy clinic where he worked. He found five distinct reactions to his counsel. They were:

INDIFFERENCE: There were a bunch of men that flatly said, "I just gave her a ride here. It's up to her if she wants to keep it. I don't want anything to do with it. It's on her." *So now it's an "it?"*

ABUSE: You recognize physical abuse because you see it; however, for emotional, financial, and verbal abuse, how can you tell it's going on? Unless you are trained or have gone through it yourself, they are the silent killers. I ask that you keep your eyes and ears open to recognize signs of any abuse and stand on the ready to offer healing through hope.

There were several cases of physical abuse, but the two that stand out in his memory were one girl who came in alone with a swollen black eye. The father of the baby had beaten her up and was arrested. The other was a girl who came in with a broken arm, and then the father of the baby left town. The sad statistic here is most women go back to the abuse instead of venturing out on their own. They do this for many reasons, but a common thread is that most do not believe they have a choice.

BULLYING: This is a silent, behind-closed-doors act of abuse. Thankfully, the courts are starting to recognize the impact of "verbal" abuse characterized as bullying. The most common form of bullying is when the father of the baby wants abortion and sends the girl to the clinic alone. He puts the girl down, demeans her and says she is worthless, telling her she couldn't survive without him. He threatens her with bodily harm, and sometimes those threats become reality. When you are verbally beaten down and told these things over and over, you start to believe them for yourself. The words become your identity and you stay stuck.

ABANDONMENT: This comes in physical, financial, and emotional forms (just like abuse). With physical abandonment, they leave. With financial abandonment, they stick around but offer no support financially, and with emotional abandonment, they just don't care and check out. These fathers who abandoned their girlfriends were out of the picture entirely. They didn't come to the clinic nor offer any support.

REGRET: There are some men who regret the abortion. As a sidewalk counselor for the 40 Days of Life campaign,[18] standing vigil across the street or next to a Planned Parenthood facility offering hope and alternatives to abortion, Dennis had run across several guys who talked about how sorry they were that they had forced the girl to abort.

UNINFORMED: How does this happen? Ignorance or lack of communication? Dennis knew a guy named Peter Shinn, who found out *after his girlfriend had the abortion* and was so distraught that he became an advocate for the unborn and founded Pro-Life Unity as well as several other pro-Life organizations.[19]

Maybe some of these responses from Dennis surprised you like they did me. I have not lived with my head in the sand, but I didn't purposely seek understanding outside of what I already knew. Does that sound familiar? My hope and prayer are that we lay aside all judgement and offer healing and help through a Christ-centered approach. Men, women, and children are hurting and in need of understanding. **Please do not be the reason someone gives up hope when it is in your power to offer it.** It is time for the Church to come together and be the hands and feet of Jesus in a way that is unprecedented. Be the light.

Chapter 4

Love Equals Validation

> Bad company corrupts good character.
> 1 Corinthians 15:33 (NIV)

I wish I could say my flow of bad choices ended here, but the trauma, the dismissive lingering effects of my abortion and the breakup with Mike was actually the catalyst of all that would follow. I did not give value to the complexity of my decisions and this was before I knew there were consequences that were far-reaching and deeply buried in my soul.

I did give "love" a try a few years after this episode. Things would be different this time around, I told myself. Different because I learned my lesson. I would heed warning signs and give credit to my intuition. I grew up in between Mike and my next relationship. But what I really did was grow calloused.

Matthew proved to be just as reckless as Mike was with our relationship. I was truly committed and was a one-man woman. I did not venture outside of my relationship. *Maybe that needed to change.* I started blaming my past failures on the other person. I did not dare reflect on the possibility I could be the problem.

But one thing I believed was that since I take myself wherever I go, if I didn't like myself, it would be impossible to truly like someone else. You can't give away what you don't have—love. This became my mantra.

Matthew, I would discover after three years of dating and an engagement ring, was also too popular and decided having more than one girlfriend at a time was his thing. He was a bodybuilder, so he had lots of fans and most were not men. Initially, I trusted him. But once again, I saw warning signs of unfaithfulness, shorter and fewer visits, rushed conversations, and constant interruptions to our plans. Even though we had privacy at his parent's place, he rarely made the effort to visit me at home. It was always me going to see him which was a warning sign I refused to acknowledge. I ignored all these things because I was sure he loved me. One night, I called several times on my way home and kept getting a busy signal (this was before call waiting). I drove myself crazy (*am I being paranoid?*) and stayed up extra late until I got through over an hour later. When the phone finally rang, he didn't answer!

When curiosity overcame my ignorance, the next time I visited him I searched for proof of my suspicions. Of course, I had to wait until he was in the shower or working on his truck. I was secretly hoping I would find nothing, while also praying for something to confirm my suspicions so I wouldn't feel crazy. We were together for five years and engaged for three of them, but I would later learn that a long engagement is a sign of a lack of commitment. He only put a ring on my finger to claim me, or to keep others away. In his bedroom, there were things that were off-limits to me even though I was his fiancée. When I didn't find anything in the "forbidden" drawer, I went and searched in his "secret" trunk. And there, under all the clothes, I found what I was hoping not to find. Several love letters, recently written, and the

Love Equals Validation

proof that he was in fact seeing at least two other women. *What did I do wrong?* I loved him, I catered to him, I was fun and outgoing and rarely disagreed with his ideas of how to spend our time. Why didn't I measure up, again? What was it about me that made these men search outside of our relationship? How could this happen again?

I started adding to my insecurities by planting seeds of unworthiness, rejection, and abandonment. I didn't understand why I was not enough. I decided to add more bricks to my wall of denial I mentioned earlier, that would prevent me from getting hurt again. It was my coping mechanism. I poured my energy into work which always seemed to validate me and drown out the negative self-image. What I didn't realize was that by putting up a wall to protect myself, I not only didn't accept love I also wasn't able to give it. So, what does one do in this situation? You look for another love to latch onto, of course.

I knew my wall would protect me, but this time my choices in men would be different. I didn't want to be alone. I yearned for a loving and nurturing relationship. We are created for relationships and have an innate longing for belonging and acceptance. **If I wasn't accepted for who I was, I reasoned, I would learn how to be what others expected.** This worked for a time. What I didn't realize was that with each failure I chose to block out the pain. This is where strongholds are born. There was a root ball developing of bitterness, stemming from self-criticism and unforgiveness which were learned behaviors triggered by disappointment and unmet needs.

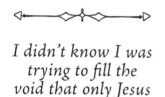

I didn't know I was trying to fill the void that only Jesus could fill.

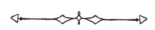

Chapter 5

From Broken to Bride

> For the time is coming when people will not endure sound teaching, but having itching ears they will accumulate for themselves teachers to suit their own passions.
> 2 Timothy 4:3 (ESV)

In both my relationships with Mike and Matthew, I was attracted to the outward appearance, and to be honest, the popularity of these men. I was familiar with the warning signs but chose to ignore them in order to stay in the relationship. I remembered being told that my suspicions were caused by my insecurity. That I was simply paranoid and jealous.

I imagined Matthew getting random phone calls from girls I didn't know saying hi with zeal on the other end. I was certain this was the reason behind our last-minute plans that were changed or canceled. I wanted to believe that my self-doubt explained the paranoia. If only that were the truth. My self-doubt was ushered in by the comments of others and I started to believe my internal dialogue, Satan's dialogue, that I wasn't worthy of love. I graduated swiftly from a naïve fifteen-year-old child to a twenty-eight-year-old woman who couldn't seem to shake the yearning for significance which I chose to rest on men.

After Mike and Matthew, I was reluctant to have a steady relationship. I opted for simple friendships to keep the prospect of romance off the table and hung out with a variety of male and female friends. I was living on my own and making excellent money. I may have been bad at relationships, but I was really good at work. Both of these extremes, bad relationships and good work ethics, were by-products of the emotional pain caused by abortion that I would learn over thirty years later. I excelled and was often given promotions and bonuses based on my performance. I realize now that recognition and attention at work helped me minimize the emptiness I felt from rejection. I was able to overlook my relationship failures by succeeding in my professional life.

I wanted to be loved so badly, that I settled for bad love.

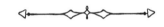

Succeeding at work helped dull the pain for a time. By focusing on what I was good at, I also prevented myself from confronting the emotional pain and turmoil in order to heal. With popularity and money to spare, I was going out every weekend and living the high life. I did not have to answer to anyone. I had it all together. But all this was just another coping mechanism to avoid facing the pain. By going out on weekends, I welcomed the distraction of noise to drown out the voices of unworthiness in my head. It was in this season that my best girlfriend took me to a party to get me out of the house. This is where I met Luke.

Luke was another charmer. He looked like the Marlboro Man and was in shape. At first, I did not notice him. I was too busy with my exclusive pity party to notice anyone, but he noticed me. He wooed me by describing what I was wearing to the DJ and my girlfriend had to tell me the DJ was describing me. This was Luke's effort to get me on the dance floor. He didn't know me or my name, so he got creative and asked the DJ for help. I had been sulking and wasn't seeking attention, so I was flattered he noticed me. I decided to dance with him; it was only a dance, for goodness' sake. I don't have to wallow in self-pity if someone had taken notice. I soon discovered his wittiness and sense of humor were very attractive to me and provided an escape from the pity party.

That innocent dance sparked my interest in dating again. It had been six months since my break-up with Matthew so that was plenty of time to get over him. What I didn't realize was that unless I dealt with my insecurities, they would follow me into every relationship I considered. Unless I dove deep to change who I was attracted to, the cycle of bad choices would continue.

We started dating. Things quickly got serious. He wanted to move back to his hometown in Arizona, where all of his family and connections were, and I thought that would be exciting. Before the move, we had a going-away party, and that is where he proposed. We lived together for six months before relocating to Tucson, and everything was beautiful. I thought I knew him.

Luke was the perfect gentleman while we were in Maryland. Once settled in Tucson, things took a turn for the worse. I was a jealous, insecure woman when Luke came into my life, and now it escalated because I was away from my tribe. At home, I had the safety net of friends that always agreed with me and never challenged my point of view. Mom tried to talk sense into me, "What's the rush, take your time, "but I naturally didn't listen because she had no idea what she was talking about, right? I was wrong again.

Luke started going out without me and one time even took the car keys and my purse so I couldn't follow him or go out myself. Can you say control? While I was "stranded" in Tucson, he became emotionally abusive and belittling. I had little to no support system and was too embarrassed to tell anyone in Maryland what was going on. I was questioning my worth once again. I started to believe I deserved whatever was happening to me and that I had no control over it. But these were lies. I also started to believe Luke's words that I needed him because I was useless. He insinuated that because I didn't have a college degree, I was stupid. That nobody else would treat me as good as he did. My prior relationships laid the groundwork for welcoming in, not openly but secretly, more lies that I would claim as truth. The messages were: "you are not good enough, I am as good as you will ever have, I love you, that's why I do the things I do, you deserve whatever happens to you, etc." The root of unworthiness was growing deeper with each thought. Once again, I managed to attach myself to the feeling of significance based on someone else's opinion of me. This was dangerous territory.

When your identity is wrapped up in what you do, what others say about you, your possessions, or your status, it will eventually fail you.

In my late thirties, I would learn that my identity theft was something I allowed to manifest. I gave those other identities permission to steal my true identity. Unless you are tethered to Christ, you have a mistaken identity. I didn't know that. I needed to be told that my significance, acceptance, and adoption into a royal family is not based on what I did or didn't do, it is simply based on whose I am. I am the daughter of a King!

That is where my identity comes from. Why did it take so long to learn this?

To say there were warning signs with Luke would be an understatement. Once again, I chose to ignore them to spare myself embarrassment. I was committed to marrying him for many reasons: his mom offered me her engagement ring, I followed him to his hometown, we had more good days than bad, and I was pregnant. I did what any rational and broken woman in this situation would do. I married him. Mom made all the arrangements and paid for the wedding. We flew back to Maryland for the festivities. It was a beautiful wedding. The guests had no idea of the masquerade behind the scenes. I am not sure I understood the magnitude of what was brewing under the happy and hearty exterior myself. I was five months pregnant as I walked down the aisle.

Two years after my daughter, Tara, was born, I had great suspicions my husband was cheating on me. Determined not to drag this out as I did with past relationships, I filed for divorce. Since I had nowhere to go in the meantime, we decided to continue sharing the marital home and ride out the thirty days it took to get divorced in Arizona. Tara and I had one side of the house, and he had the other. When the thirty days passed, I flew my dad out to help with the drive back home. With a two-year-old in tow, we loaded a U-Haul and drove cross-country. Once we were in Maryland, I asked dad to stop so I could get out of the truck and kiss the ground. I paid homage to this momentous event by getting a personalized license plate for my car with the letters: BMORE, which I've had for over twenty-five years.

But the divorce began another downward spiral.

Plagued once again with self-doubt, unworthiness, why me, and the biggest questions swirling around in my head: "What is it about me that makes men seek out other women?" and "When do you know you are enough?" It was like a replay of my prior relationship failures, only this time there was a child in the picture and more at stake. I had to keep it together for my daughter's sake. I started reconnecting with old friends that I lost touch with while in Arizona. I was starting over but my new life would carry old mindsets, a recipe for disaster. The familiar noise of my internal dialogue, plagued with self-doubt and unworthiness, confirmed that my insecurities would be my companion for a long time. Deep inside I was hurting. I was afraid I would always be alone and unsure if anyone would want me. I was putting all my energy into work once again. Work became my survival mechanism.

Looking back now, I wanted to be wanted so badly and to know I had someone in my life that I ignored the warning signs that were so prevalent. I was ignorant, arrogant, and full of pride. I had an impenetrable heart. Because I didn't know the Lord, I settled for any marriage instead of waiting for the right one. I kept the persona that all was wonderful, and life was better than I'd ever known it to be. I had taken my past hurts and perceptions of myself, and of marriage in general, into my marriage with Luke and didn't realize what harm that would do. I had no idea why I continued to do what I didn't want to do. It was like what Paul described in Romans 7:18b–19, "For I have the desire to do what is right, but not the ability to carry it out. For I do not do the good I want, but the evil I do not want is what I keep on doing" (ESV). I also didn't know that my behavior and how I

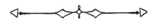

I used marriage as a temporary fix to a problem I had not identified and didn't want to dive deep to figure out.

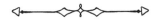

saw the world were linked to my past abortion. If you ignore it, it will go away, right? Once again, I was wrong.

Chapter 6

The Masquerade Charade

> Today I have given you the choice between life and death, between blessings and curses. Now I call on heaven and earth to witness the choice you make. Oh, that you would choose life, so that you and your descendants might live!
> Deuteronomy 30:19 (NLT)

Although society challenges the sacredness of marriage, I did not get married with the intention of getting divorced. It seems we live in a world where the fairy tale of marriage, kids, and the white picket fence has been replaced by the hustle and bustle of the concrete jungle and the rise to the top. This is for men and women alike. The feminist movement, in my opinion, hurt women more than it helped them. We have forgotten our roots. Our roles have become blurred. We have forgotten how God designed us with unique gifts and talents to serve one another and His church.

I was living by "worldly standards" and had no desire to live any differently. I rejected the idea that there was a God, and especially one that cared about me which, I believed, was confirmed, and compounded by my divorce.

The military has something called Mine-Resistant, Ambush-Protected equipment. The mask I wore was "**mind**-resistant, ambush-protected equipment" which I practiced to protect my heart. My thoughts were held captive, but not as they should be (2 Corinthians 10:5). There seemed to be a chasm ever widening between the reality of who I thought I was and whose I was. I pretended I wanted the divorce. I pretended it didn't hurt, and I accepted that I would be alone again. But I had to find a way to stop the pain of failure and rejection.

After all I had been through, if there was a God, I didn't want any part of Him. Thank goodness, God loves us and chases us down whether we like it or not!

I did have enough common sense to purchase a home for me and Tara with the settlement that I had to battle for from the divorce. I could have easily squandered it all away. When I look back on this season, I can clearly see God's hands all over it, and this was before I had anything to do with Him. Because He is love, He finds a way to bless us in the messes. God protected me by giving me wisdom beyond my comprehension. Once on solid footing in Maryland, I settled into a new rhythm. I buried what happened and shut down the questions as soon as someone started prying into the events that led up to us returning home. It was nobody's business.

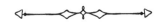

On the outside I was strong, unmoved, and put together, on the inside I was falling apart.

In an attempt to suppress the feelings of loss, I started using cocaine introduced to me by my younger brother before I met

Luke. I dabbled in it before moving to Arizona but was clean while I lived there because I had no connections in Arizona for the drug. I was now getting reacquainted with what would become a weekend addiction.

I would later learn that these coping mechanisms, along with others, were prevalent in women who have had an abortion. Post Abortive Syndrome is medically recognized today. Some of the symptoms are drug or alcohol abuse (check), promiscuity (check), avoiding close relationships (check), depression (check), etc. I had all the symptoms but no way to address or recover from them. There were no post-abortive studies available (shoot, there wasn't even a name for it back then). Abortion, by its very nature, was not something you ever talked about. It turns out I was becoming the "normal" post-abortive case study. It never dawned on me all these years later that that was the reason I was in such pain.

I was numbing the pain of my failures with cocaine and alcohol on a pretty regular basis, BUT YOU WOULD NEVER KNOW IT, because of the mask I wore.

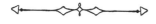

I had a decent work ethic but an unfocused moral barometer. I figured if being the one-man woman wasn't working, I might as well throw caution to the wind and lower my standards, which was not characteristic of me. It was as if I had to prove something to myself: I could be just as callous as the men I'd chosen. In this maddening phase, I felt alone and yet, I was completely dismissive of having a meaningful relationship. I was chasing easy by discounting my worth. It is only in looking in the rearview mirror of this part of my journey, that I can recognize the God of all creation protecting me and Tara without adding insult to injury.

May this prove to those who are confused and still kicking the tire on God and faith that He is merciful. He withholds what we deserve, and graciously gives us what we don't deserve.

Now that I was living in my hometown, I had family and friends as a support system, and I had built-in babysitters. With no shortage of sitters and money from a good job, it was a perfect opportunity to get into trouble. I was running away from being a mom to Tara to escape the pain of the child I chose death for. Having my mom available to babysit any time made it easy for me to come and go as I pleased and not dwell on the pain in my life. She was making up for the two years she missed out on while I was away in Arizona. I didn't understand at the time how my absence took away the opportunity for her to be supportive and involved in my pregnancy and delivery. I didn't realize how much that broke her heart. I misunderstood the impact my actions had on someone else, namely my mom.

During this season, my younger brother, Randy, was imprisoned for writing counterfeit checks. He was always testing fate and it finally caught up to him. I was very close to him and it broke my heart, but at the same time I had no compassion for him since he caused it. This exchange is significant as it will bear testimony to a future event. We were home for about six months and my sister, to help me get over the embarrassment of a failed marriage, decided to throw a "Divorce Party" for me. This was where I met my second husband, Chad. We dated, he moved into my house, and we were married within a year. I was so thrilled that someone else would want me. I suppose I fast-tracked this man, in case he changed his mind. There were serious warning signs throughout our relationship, same as with my first husband, but I dismissed them because he "loved" me and Tara. (I mean, he bought Tara her first bike. That's love, right? By now, my standards were pretty low.)

The Masquerade Charade

me and Tara at her dance recital

me, Mom and Tara in TX

I married Luke out of fear of letting others down and to spare embarrassment, and now I would do the same thing all over again with Chad. How absurd was that! What was it in me that thought I had to settle? That I was not worthy of authentic, no-strings-attached love? I really did not know what that was. If you don't know what you are looking for, how will you know if you ever find it? Why did I see myself as deserving of whatever I got? How do you ignore clear warning signs that marriage might not be the right choice for you, again? I needed the love-sized hole in my heart filled and made whole, and I thought marriage would do that. I was wanted—that was what mattered to me. Do you see a theme here?

I received a phone call from my brother, Randy, in prison. It was early in the morning and I am not a morning person, so I was short with him. He said, "Mouse, I am going to die before Mom and Dad do." I yelled at him and showed no compassion. I was angry with him for speaking such nonsense. Within six months he called again. Whenever he called me from prison, I would debate whether to accept the charges (they were always collect calls) and then I would try to speed up the conversation to spare getting a huge phone bill. He said he was sending me a book I needed to read, "for my own good." *OK, so now he was trying to teach me?* He said he had been "born again" (I had no idea what that even meant), and that he needed me to know Jesus. His words went in one ear and out the other. I was proud and always judging his motives. I discounted what he said and chalked it up to him being bored and finding a different way to pass the time. I told him I'd read it (which I had no intention of doing), reminding him that I didn't believe in Jesus and didn't believe he did either. Thank the Lord, my rejection didn't stop my brother from continuing the dialogue.

What I didn't understand was what it took to actually send anything from "inside." You had to be in good graces with the prison staff, have the finances to send something, and the tenacity to pursue it. Often Randy would tell me he sent a letter and it would take weeks and sometimes months to receive it. It was not as simple as going to the post office to drop something off. It was complicated and cumbersome. The same held true for him receiving mail. Mail was searched, opened, and money would go missing. There was nothing anyone could do about it. I can remember my disbelief when he would tell me he didn't receive a letter or the stamps and money I sent. I was so used to Randy's history of manipulation; I discounted the thought that he was telling me the truth.

When I got the book, *Equal Time* by N. Ted Smith,[20] which Randy inscribed, I opened the package and immediately packed it away. I had zero interest in opening the book beyond the inscription page. That book, that I now cherish, sat in a moving box for over twelve years! I look now at this book on my shelf with gratitude, holding back tears at his inscription to me. I have tried to imagine what was going through his mind as he methodically highlighted areas he didn't want me to miss. Did he pray for me with each stroke? What I held in my hand, that I didn't know then, was a reminder of Randy's heart for me. It was a reminder of his love for me even through my ridicule and rejection. He was attempting to win my soul for Jesus (Mark 16:15-18). There are prison ministries all over the world for reaching the lost souls **inside** the prison walls (one of which is called Prison Fellowship[21] that I was a part of). But it is not often, and especially in 1993, that you heard of the reversal. Randy was ahead of the times.

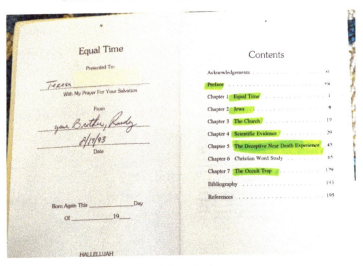

Book inscription

2 Timothy 3:15 says, *"and how from childhood* you have been acquainted with the sacred writings, which are able to make you wise for salvation through faith in Christ Jesus" (ESV; emphasis mine). My introduction to the Christian faith in childhood family gatherings, of which I was unaware at the time, made an impact on me even though I was not paying attention. Whether we learn of Jesus purposefully or not, if we are surrounded by those that are active in their Christian faith, we will reap a benefit. The very next verse, 2 Timothy 3:16, was the last scripture Randy highlighted in the book to make sure I didn't miss it. "All Scripture is breathed out by God and profitable for teaching, for reproof, for correction, and for training in righteousness." Turns out he was telling the truth when he said he would die before Mom and Dad. Three years after I received his book, Randy died alone in prison. He was thirty-two. (I love and miss you every day, Randy. Say "hi" to Mom for me.)

The Masquerade Charade

Me and Randy at Sabino Canyon Seven Falls

Santa Monica (80's), heading out to dance in Santa Monica

Randy's Family

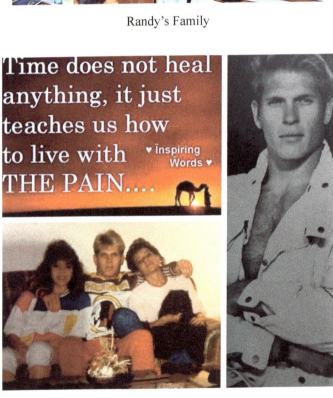

Randy's Memorial Announcement

Before I married my second husband, Chad, we discussed having children, but it was a very shallow discussion. I already had Tara and was quite content. She was six and I survived the single parenting season and now had a very comfortable rhythm. I said, "I will give it one month after we are married and if I am not pregnant, it is not meant to be." Who did I think I was? This is a good time to remind you that the Lord directs our steps. Turns out, we didn't need a month. In His infinite wisdom, I became pregnant on our honeymoon. I will share that this pregnancy, although somewhat planned, was scary on so many levels. I had been content with my one child. The Lord decided to shake things up a little and bless us with twin girls. Who can understand the mysteries of the Lord?

But with our blessing, I would be shaken even more. The twins were premature. This was a new test for me. When I learned that the girls were each under 3 lb. and would not be coming home with me, I had a meltdown. I was sent home a few days after an emergency C-section that I did not want, and the twins remained in NICU (neonatal intensive care unit) until they were healthy enough to come home. I still didn't know the Lord, had no desire to get to know Him (I was still chasing easy), but He was, I would realize later, chasing after me.

To delay the start of my maternity leave, I asked my boss, Louise, if I could work from home until the girls were sent home. I wanted to start the leave clock then, giving me a full six weeks once they were home. She did not hesitate to grant my wish. Reflecting on this season, I can see how the Lord, whom I had zero interest in, was interested in me. He orchestrated the unfolding of these events. Six weeks went by. I traveled daily to the hospital after work and had the recommended "skin to skin" time, while also feeding them breastmilk through a tube.

The day they finally came home on monitors, I was able to be with them for my entire six-week maternity leave.

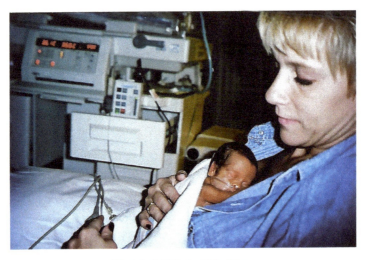

Hospital Skin to Skin Time

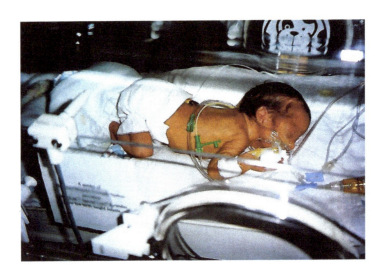

The Masquerade Charade

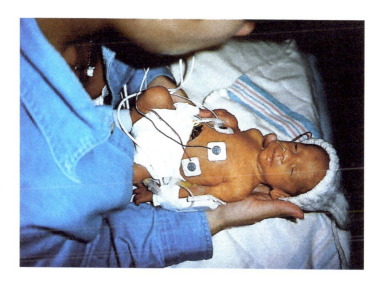

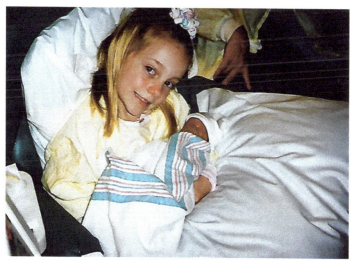

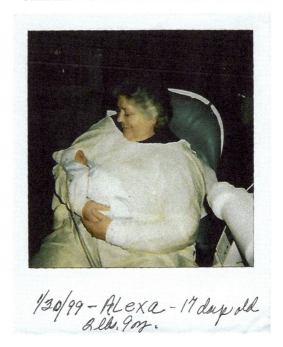

1/30/99 – Alexa – 17 day old
2 lbs. 9 oz.

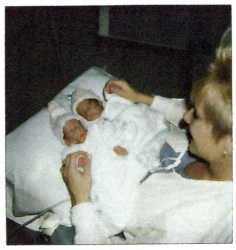

Alexa & Alyssa 2/5/99

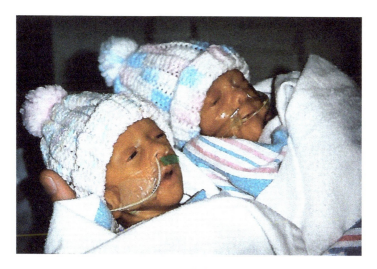

Hospital Time

Tara 11, Twins 3

Christmas 2016

I would like to tell you that I fell to my knees and prayed without ceasing for the health of my girls and their full and complete recovery, but I didn't. I'd like to say that I didn't operate in my own strength. But I did. I'd like to say that I had a prayer team interceding on our behalf, but I didn't. I didn't know the Lord like that, and probably even blamed Him for the less than perfect start of the twins' lives. I do remember being angry. *Why me?* Even when I realized the girls would not only survive but thrive, I did not give thanks or credit to the One who sustained us through this stressful and tiresome season. I wonder how this season might have been different if I was going through it with the Lord? But in reality, even when I didn't see it, feel it, or know it, He was there. Thank you, my sweet Lord and Savior.

We were now a family of five and my husband was the odd man out. He lived in a sea of estrogen. On the outside, my life seemed complete. However, after the trauma of both my brother Randy's death, and the premature birth of my twins, I was once again looking for comfort. My husband was never home and when he was, he was abusive emotionally, financially, and even once physically. I started getting high again and drinking on the weekends. I was miserable, but I didn't know what to do about it. No one was speaking into me the life that I so desperately needed. But to be fair, I wasn't seeking it out either.

A year later, we moved into a new home and it was there, in this new community, that God found me by way, of all things, a hairdresser.

Part 2

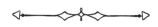

Adoption and Redemption

Chapter 7

The Foundation of Faith

> For by him all things were created, in heaven and on earth, visible and invisible, whether thrones or dominions or rulers or authorities—all things were created through him and for him. Colossians 1:16 (ESV)

> Before I formed you in the womb I knew you, before you were born I set you apart; I appointed you as a prophet to the nations. Jeremiah 1:5 (NIV)

On one hand, the reality of these verses can catch me off guard. If He created all things and all things are through Him, why do we have such evil and destruction in the world? Why does it seem like the righteous suffer while the evil prospers? The simple answer is this: humans have **free will**. Again, this points us back to the "choices" dilemma. And if I was known and set apart before I was born, how did He know I would actually follow Him with all the choices not to? Oh, the mysteries of God. I have a laundry list of questions when I see Him. Such lavish love He extends to us all.

On the other hand, I can also find great comfort in these verses. Knowing that His ways and thoughts are not like mine (thank goodness) means that the mystery of God allows us to wrestle with our current reality in a way that also honors His good and perfect will. Ultimately, He does use everything for our good (Romans 8:28)!

Mine is not a fairy tale journey laced with inexplicable joy, rather it is a lingering obsession to do things my way that provided lots of switchbacks to navigate along the way to finding true freedom—freedom in Christ. I was always the little girl who needed to be the best at whatever I did and that carried through to adulthood.

I was raised by well-meaning, loving parents who were themselves spiritually depleted. I went to Sunday school against my will. I saw it as a form of babysitting for my parents since I never remember seeing them at church. My younger brother, younger sister, and I were dropped off and then picked up when Sunday school was over. There was no discussion of or reflection on the lessons afterwards, nor were there any visible signs of practicing or witnessing their faith. When I was ten or eleven, and old enough to not be afraid to voice my opinion, I asked to stay home from Sunday school, and it was granted. With the freedom to sleep in on Sundays, that's exactly what I did.

Other than the early exposure to "church," I had no real witness during my late teens to early 30s. The only significant religious experiences I had, aside from weddings and funerals, were from extended family members. I used to watch my favorite Aunt Patty interact with everyone at family functions. She had that gentle and quiet spirit that I now long for, but I didn't give it a name back then. She taught Sunday school, and does to this day, and loved children which was quite evident to everyone she met.

I can remember her coming to my rescue when my mean boy cousins would pick on me or not include me in any of their games. I adore my cousins today, but when we went camping and they finally included me in the "woods" game, I didn't know it was a game to leave me alone in the woods to find my way back to the campsite on my own (I did, eventually). It scared me out of my mind! With Aunt Patty, I always felt so loved and accepted. To this day, she is my favorite aunt. What is amazing to me is that she has been married for over 60 years to a man who has never accompanied her to church for worship. About five years ago, I asked her why my dad, her brother, would never go to church and that's when she revealed that my Uncle Red, her husband, didn't either. I was shocked! In the back of my mind, I thought how that must hurt her heart to know they were not "equally yoked" and that her spiritual head of household was remiss in his duties. However, I now understand what Paul taught the Corinthians that the unbelieving spouse is sanctified through the believing husband or wife. That's reassuring. Back in those days, when you got married, you stayed married. Divorce was not an option. Much like with my parents.

Once, I asked my dad why he didn't go to church, and he told me that Grandma forced him to go every Sunday where he was the bell ringer to chime the start of the Baptist service. Although he left the house neat and clean, by the time he got to church he was a mess. He didn't think about the time, running through the mud and dirt to get there, and was often very late. The whole experience of church left him frustrated and he wanted nothing to do with it when he got older.

As a young child, my Grandma Hughes was a beautiful soul to me. I remembered visiting her in Pennsylvania and walking in the house to the sweet aroma of sticky buns tickling my nose or the warm tantalizing smell of homemade mouthwatering bread. I loved and enjoyed both. Of course, we kids preferred the gooey, make-a-mess-on-your-hands-and-face sticky buns. The sad part is this recipe left our family heritage when she went home to glory (I love you, Grandma). It was much later in life that I learned she was the disciplinarian and Pappy just went along with her. There is a trail of strong women in my background which I can relate to.

There were other family members that I remembered being called on to say grace at our crowded Thanksgiving dinners. There were usually seventy-five of us, and even as a little girl, I remembered my grandma and my Uncle Fred saying grace. I couldn't always follow their prayers, but I knew to bow my head and be still. There was a sense of peace and warmth that I recognized when all of us held hands for Thanksgiving grace. The generations have come, and some are gone on to glory, but I am grateful for the legacy my grandma left. We have carried on the Hughes tradition through the generations. I used to despise the long drive, cold weather, getting up early, dressing up, and being cooped up in a car with my sister and brother. But now I have come to cherish it.

Thanksgiving

Family Reunion

Because of the coronavirus, the world was on notice to forgo gatherings outside of your household. In the interest of limiting the spread, we heeded the warnings of the CDC (Centers for Disease Control) and did not gather for Thanksgiving in 2020. This was the first time in my adult life we had not met. I have an even greater appreciation and sensitivity to this beloved tradition. This too, came down to a choice. Would I honor the authorities or my own selfish ambition?

While we are a typical messed-up family, my mature years have taught me to savor these memories and hold fast to the love of family, mess and all. It was my early introductions to faith, I realized later, that would shape my future. Maybe like me, you did not come from a religious background; it would be something that developed over time. It wasn't until much later in life that I realized the path before me and those that spoke into my life were what weaved the tapestry of my journey.

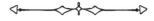

The innocence of these years would soon be swallowed up by the reckless, self-centered living that would follow; however, NOT ONE experience was wasted. God has used all of my tangled messes to create something beautiful that would point others to Him.

I am confident that I had family praying for my salvation and although some are not here to witness the answer, I will see them again when I am escorted to heaven. If you are someone who grew up in a Christian home and have honored your early teaching, you are blessed. Whether you loved church or not, it was hard for me, which is why I rebelled and chased the easy way for far too long. What an incredible lesson I learned that it's never too late to turn back to the lover of your soul. He loves me whether I like it or not! And I didn't like it until my early thirties.

Chapter 8

When His Love Found Me

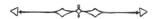

The Lord appeared to us in the past, saying: "I have loved you with an everlasting love; I have drawn you with unfailing kindness."
Jeremiah 31:3 (NIV)

Who shall separate us from the love of Christ? Shall trouble or hardship or persecution or famine or nakedness or danger or sword?
Romans 8:35

In His unconventional method of getting my attention, God used a hairdresser to change the trajectory of my life forever. God is crazy good like that and very unpredictable. Of course, I am not discounting the foundation of faith witnessed at Thanksgiving dinners early on, or the brave attempt by Randy from prison to draw my attention outside of myself. I had to be ready and open to receive the gift of salvation, and the Lord brought it to me by way of a sassy, short haircut.

Dawn was a hairdresser who lived in our neighborhood, and I was looking for convenience and expertise, so I called and scheduled an appointment. While leaning my head back in her washbasin, I looked up at the base of the upper cabinet, and there was a piece of paper that said, "Even the hairs on your head are numbered." Piquing my interest, I asked her what that meant. She shared, with joy and excitement, the truth of the gospel and this Jesus who saves. I was intrigued and curious. Is this the same Jesus Randy tried to introduce me to? Is it the same Jesus we ended our Thanksgiving prayers with? I was fixing to find out.

Dawn had a pamphlet on her counter that intrigued me. It was an invitation to a women's retreat in Pennsylvania. Not being the shy type, I invited myself. I told Chad I was going away to the retreat and knowing his controlling behavior would try to stop me, I arranged for my mom to watch Tara that weekend, in case he did try to. I then called my cousin, Lisa, who lived in Pennsylvania, and asked her to join me. She said yes and the three of us, Dawn, Lisa, and me, shared a room. It was the second day of the retreat that the Lord arrested my heart and I gave it to Him! I accepted Jesus as my personal Lord and Savior in 2001.

retreat in PA

Me and Lisa at the retreat.

Miraculously, after being addicted to cocaine for many years, I was healed from its powerful grip. I felt lighter. I was peaceful and calm. Lisa, who had on a few previous occasions tried to talk to me about the Christian faith, told me she had been praying all along for my salvation. Her faithful prayers had finally been answered. I was on fire for Jesus. I was so excited, I wanted to share Jesus with my husband and anyone else I encountered. I wanted others to experience the joy of salvation I personally witnessed.

Much to my chagrin, my husband didn't want to hear about it. He continued to live the life we lived prior to my commitment to Jesus. This led to marital conflict. The Lord held me up during those tumultuous years and I relied heavily on His peace. I used this time to find a church home, get involved, and find ways to serve the lover of my soul. Remember the little girl who had to be the best at what she did? I was now applying that to my spiritual walk.

My church home brought me God-fearing friends who are, to this day, interwoven in my life. These wise women of the word continually speak into my life. I served on the hospitality and drama teams at church and served with the Christian Motorcycle Association (CMA).[22] I started a haphazard practice of devotions from *Our Daily Bread*.[23] I wanted to help spread the Good News and if I couldn't do it at home or with my immediate family, who were skeptical about my Christian conversion, then I would do it where people might listen. The friends I met at CMA broke off and created their own ministry called Praise-n-Thunder Outreach Ministries (PNTOM).[24] I followed them to the new ministry and was voted in as vice president. I loved the energy at the meetings and the fieldwork. We went into prisons, secular motorcycle events, and did "church crashes." You've heard of wedding crashers, right? We were motorcycle riders showing up to bless and tithe at a church we didn't belong to. We did community outreach, and to this day, continue to have a strong homeless ministry, run by an ever-faithful servant of the Lord named Henry.

I was able to convince my husband, Chad, to join me on some of the motorcycle rides but for the most part, I was on my own. When Chad did participate, I acted in a way I knew pleased him which was contrary to my new Christian identity. I didn't want him to be uncomfortable around a bunch of Bible-believing, Christ followers, so I downplayed my belief and even shunned the Lord (like Peter did in John 18:25–27) to gain favor with my husband. Ridiculous, right?

One of the women at a motorcycle event was brave enough to pull me aside and tell me I seemed confused. I asked her what she meant by that. Mary said I seem to be confused because what I wore and how I carried myself around Chad was not the same Teresa that showed up at church or Christian events. She pointed out the revealing biker garb I was wearing and rebuked me for it. Someone had once reprimanded her when she wore revealing clothes and she was paying it forward to help me see what I was doing. I immediately understood what she meant and thanked her for her willingness to speak up. Although it took courage, her gentle "course correction" was an invaluable lesson I am so grateful for.

I was very conscientious from that point forward to honor the Lord with my dress and demeanor. I had been trying to live with one foot in the world—to appeal to man—and the other in the Word. I was doing what the book of Revelation warns us about being lukewarm, "So, because you are lukewarm, and neither hot nor cold, *I will spit you out of my mouth"* (Revelation 3:16 ESV; emphasis mine). Until writing this, I didn't compare this 3:16 verse to one of the most famous verses found in John 3:16, "For God so loved the world, that he gave his only begotten Son, so that we may have *everlasting life.*" These seem to be exact opposites. What Mary did for me was show me that both of these verses are equally true. In other words, she uncovered a "blind spot" for me. Through God's infinite wisdom and mercy, He will link arms with the people that we need in our lives to help fulfill His purpose.

Chad and I were going in opposite directions and eventually separated. I learned an important lesson in this experience. I could not lead my husband to the Lord if he wasn't ready. Yes, he was sanctified through my faith, but he was not receiving any teaching. Why? Mainly because I thought it was my job. I would read the Bible to him, leave Scripture highlighted on the table where he would see it, plan Christian events and gatherings. My strategic attempts probably caused him to rebel more which went against the very thing I was trying to accomplish: his personal discovery of a life with Jesus as his Lord and Savior. I struggled with the decision to separate because, as a baby Christian, I understood that Jesus hated divorce. Separation was leading to divorce. Now I can add "bad Christian" to my list of failures. Would I ever get it right?

During the separation, my husband was in a near-fatal motorcycle accident. With the Lord and prayer warriors on my side, he survived and made a full recovery. Although we were separated, I felt a strong desire to take him back in and care for him as a wife should. This was strictly a caregiver arrangement and I acted more out of guilt than for a desire to fulfill my wifely duties. *What would people think if I didn't care enough to help heal him back to health?* As a new Christian, I was sparing my reputation by taking him in. My motivation was self-serving, not honoring him, our marriage, or God. Doing the right thing, but with impure motives, does not honor God.

For four months I nursed Chad back to health. In an attempt at reconciliation, after he was healed, we took a vacation as husband and wife. Sure, our marriage was on-again, off-again, and it was off when he had his accident, but I justified in my mind that there was nothing wrong with trying to reconcile; he was still my husband and we were still married. But the reconciliation failed. And three months later, even though I had been on birth control, I learned I was pregnant.

I was broken, beat down, and had zero confidence in how to go forward. I felt trapped, helpless, humiliated, and empty. Yes, I was a Christian, but did I really know what that meant? I had stayed in a toxic relationship thinking I was honoring the Lord. I knew the Lord hates divorce (Malachi 2:16), but my lack of understanding of the context of this verse skewed the truth for my situation. I was living with my three girls in a modest home I purchased when Chad and I separated and sold our marital home, and I was working full time to provide for my family. I was getting no financial help from my husband.

Lord, how could you let this happen? I was confused. What were my options? How could I possibly handle another baby? Once again, I sought "wise" counsel. But this time, I was not shy about the pregnancy and truly wanted to do what was best for everyone, or so I thought. Although I had already experienced the aftermath of an abortion and had three young girls at home, I didn't know what to do. I confided in my mother who told me to have an abortion. I confided in Chad, my soon to be ex-husband, who told me to have an abortion. I played my life's movie trying to keep up with the demands of a typical day as a single mom with work, home, and three girls, and then played it again by adding a newborn. I was overwhelmed and these were just the planning stages. I began to give the advice of my mom and Chad some serious consideration.

Led by the Spirit, I called my friend, Dawn, who had escorted me to the retreat where I invited Christ into my life less than a year earlier. She was a Christian counselor and an excellent listener. I proceeded to share my dilemma and after a few moments of awkward silence, and lots of sniffles on my part, I was hoping she would agree that abortion was what was best. She knew how damaged I felt, how destroyed I was over another failed marriage, and how worthless, scared, confused, and drained I was from all the chaos in my life. Surely bringing another child into the mix of an already strained and dysfunctional environment would not be in the best interest of me, my girls, or the baby.

By this time, I knew what an abortion was, how it was performed, the callousness of the act, and that it was murder in the first degree. However, I was chasing easy with my justification to abort rather than to birth a child into the current dread of reality I was living. I did not have the emotional capacity to care for another child. I was doing the best I could with the three I already had and thank goodness for my mom and sister who helped with them. I simply couldn't do it. I held my breath until she finally responded.

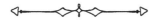

I shook my fists and looked up at God; I was angry. I didn't understand how, after chasing me down for nearly forty years and finally getting my attention, He could turn his back on me.

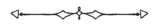

Through her own tears she asked, "Have you ever considered adoption?" I immediately shut down and exclaimed that there was no way I could ever do such a thing. I was infuriated. *Give my child away?* What a ridiculous, outrageous suggestion! I immediately thought about my position as a manager overseeing twenty-three staff members. How would I explain carrying a child to term and then giving that child away? Not to mention, I visited clients on a regular basis and they, too, would have questions, questions I didn't want to answer if it made me look bad. Just as I did with the abortion when I was fifteen, I was more concerned with what other people would think than what might potentially be best. I thought Dawn cared about me and my turmoil. *Didn't she sense how fragile I was!* What she was suggesting would completely expose me and tarnish my reputation. I questioned our friendship at this point. I didn't want to hear her adoption idea anymore and nearly hung up on her.

Once again, my identity was wrapped up in the pattern of relying on what other people thought about me. Yes, I was a Christian, but that had no bearing on what I was facing now, or did it? I fell into the societal trap of thinking it was my body and my choice. That abortion only hurt **me**, and that it was more acceptable, dinner-table discussion almost, than the *unloving* option of adoption. Once again, I was chasing easy in a hard life decision. I wrestled with the brutality of abortion, but I also couldn't see myself carrying a child for nine months and then giving it away. Why, after having these same pre-Christian thoughts at fifteen, were they eerily similar now? I began the rational phase of a crisis. How would I know who the parents truly were? That the child would be safe? That she wouldn't be abused? (Surely abortion was the ultimate abuse.) These were the thoughts that were vying for position in my mind to help me justify another abortion.

What I wanted for this baby—a loving, nurturing, and safe environment—I could not provide. I wanted to stay home and take care of this child, for him or her to lack nothing, and for the child to have a mom **and** a dad. But it couldn't be. I felt I had finally healed from the abortion over twenty-five years ago and I was considering it again? What was wrong with me? You see, I knew and understood that whatever answer I was seeking, I would find the supporting argument to qualify it.

I am confused, Lord! Where are you, God? Answer me! I thought life would make sense when I gave my heart to you? Nothing was making sense. *I thought life would be easier with you ordering my steps.* Nothing was easier. I felt persecuted. I was anxious and felt guilty considering my options and leaning towards abortion. *Hadn't I been through enough at this point in my life? What kind of test was this? Help me.*

After I calmed down, I was waiting for Dawn to say, "Just kidding, I didn't mean to mention that. Of course, you can't bring a new baby into your situation." When that didn't happen, I thought she might apologize, especially after witnessing how upset the mere suggestion of adoption made me. That didn't happen either. Instead, she allowed the awkward silence to settle, not apologizing or adding dialogue, giving me time to wrestle with my thoughts, simply being still so I could hear the voice of God speak into the situation.

But I was convinced that abortion was the right thing to do. It was best for everyone. I could go on with my life's rhythm without adding more chaos to it. I felt pressured, once again, to take care of "it." Only this time I knew "it" was a baby. After days and days of handwringing, wrestling thoughts, and sleepless nights, I booked the appointment for the abortion. I convinced myself I would be okay, everything would be okay, and life would go on as normal.

Chapter 9

Make God Choices, Not Just Good Choices

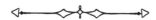

> So do not fear, for I am with you; do not be dismayed, for I am your God. I will strengthen you and help you; I will uphold you with my righteous right hand.
> Isaiah 41:10 (NIV)

> I praise you because I am fearfully and wonderfully made; your works are wonderful, I know that full well. My frame was not hidden from you when I was made in the secret place when I was woven together in the depths of the earth, your eyes saw my unformed body. All the days ordained for me were written in your book before one of them came to be.
> Psalm 139:14–16

The scheduled abortion day came. I wasn't okay. Nothing about this would be okay. *Would it ever be okay not to be okay?* I drove alone. This was something I had to do by myself. I was too proud to allow a friend to come along for moral support and comfort, too proud to be vulnerable and transparent revealing my flaws. I just wanted it to be over. I believe God wanted me to be alone. He does some of his best work in the stillness of His presence, however uncomfortable it might be for us.

I felt no peace. To overcome this sensation, I tried to drown out the doubt and follow through with my decision, much like I did with my first abortion over thirty-five years earlier. I was chasing easy and chose to ignore that the reason for my lack of peace was directly related to the lack of sound, moral, and God-honoring judgment. I was acting out of fear. As I was driving to the abortion office, the Lord spoke gently and clearly to my heart through His Spirit:

God said to me, "This is my child. I have plans for my baby. I have already picked the perfect parents. You need to trust me."

Trust you? Where were you when I got pregnant? How did you let this happen? I was on birth control for goodness' sake! God knew the desires of my heart were to please Him, angry or not. After living my life my way for so long, when the seed of faith was planted in my heart, it fell on good soil. This is what I would call blind faith. I was about five minutes from the building where the doctor would end the innocent life of my baby, when something I cannot explain happened. During this silent exchange in my heart with the God of the universe, I was directed to pull over. "Jesus take the wheel" literally happened. Once safely on the side of the road, I began to shake and cry uncontrollably. I am not sure how long I was there, it may have been ten minutes, but it felt like hours to me. *What was going on?* I questioned my sanity. Exhausted, I finally surrendered to His will. My shoulders relaxed, and what felt like the first time in years, I exhaled. I was still sobbing. God would be my refuge and my strength. I had to tell Dawn and apologize to her.

I did a U-bolt, turned around and headed home. I had no idea how this would unfold but I trusted the One who did. Once back home, I had to decide how I was going to tell Dawn, my parents, my sister, Chad, and my three girls about my decision. I called Dawn first because if she had not mentioned adoption, I am certain between the options of parenting and abortion, I would have chosen abortion. My reasoning was simple: if I thought my life was unmanageable with one child at fifteen, I certainly knew my life would be even more so now with three children. It seemed abortion was an open and shut case. If it were not for the gnawing feeling of unrest in my soul, I may have ended this life repeating the heartache of my abortion at fifteen.

Dawn was moved to tears that I chose adoption. She not only prayed over me right then, she continued to pray and sent encouraging and uplifting notes throughout my adoption journey. Dawn spoke life into me and reassured me of God-sized favor for my obedience. She told me her initial reaction to the news of my pregnancy was, "Now that you have given your life to Christ, this was going to be a true test of your new commitment to Him." She knew it would be hard for me raising and providing for three girls, ages ten and twins at four, and the recent and final split with

God's way = life always.

my ex-husband, Chad, the father of our unborn baby. She said it was imperative that she spoke truth into my life.

The Lord prepared Dawn for this moment in my life through the sin of her own abortion. The guilt she dealt with was unbearable. The weight of her sin was great, the grief was even greater. She wanted to spare me the consequences of another abortion.

Dawn didn't know then, and I later found out, that over 60% of all abortions are from professing Christians.[25] I asked Dawn what Scripture came to mind when she told me to consider adoption. She said, "Psalm 139:13–15, that God formed your little one and knit her together in your womb and the Lord was to be praised for this little gift because she is fearfully and wonderfully made. Her frame was made in the secret place and her frame was not hidden." I pray you have a friend in your circles bold enough to speak life and truth into you. Especially when what they have to say is not popular.

My parents did not handle the news well. My dad temporarily disowned me. "It's not a puppy; you don't give it away," he said. My mom was heartbroken and even offered to raise her grandchild herself as opposed to me giving her away. I felt rejected and abandoned. They didn't know what to do with my choice of adoption and I didn't know how to deal with their disappointment and disapproval. They already witnessed how difficult it was for me to raise three girls and hold down a full-time job on my own. How could they possibly think I was equipped to raise another child or see her being raised by my mom? There was little to no discussion between us, only misunderstanding and pain from both sides.

Overall, I was met with rejection, abandonment, and the denial of acceptance and love (that I thought I had long since recovered from in my past but hadn't). All the old lies from the past were resurfacing at a record pace. "You messed up," along with other thoughts of inadequacy, failure, and disappointment flooded my mind inviting me to live once again in the mistakes of my past. I faced disapproval, family that suggested adopting my child, those that didn't understand the concept, and those that outright disagreed. Then there were those who tried to push their own agenda and even some that completely walked away to avoid the reality altogether. This was my "support" system and one of the most difficult times in my life. But I decided I would give it to God, and let Him restore the joy of my soul.

I did have tremendous support from my sister and several friends. God will bring the people into your life that you need, when you need them. Through His Holy Spirit, God will sustain you and do your bidding for you. Relax and trust in the One who made you. He will make all things new again. "And the one sitting on the throne said, "Look, I am making everything new!" And then he said to me, "Write this down, for what I tell you is trustworthy and true" (Revelation 21:5 NLT).

The people you love need the freedom to process their pain and confusion in their own way.

My ex-husband did not agree with the adoption plan (but he was not in a position to parent the child, either). His reluctance was a reason for concern, as I needed him to agree to the plan. In my state of residence, the father must agree to and sign the legally binding adoption papers. I was trusting God to change his heart. I was praying it would be soon.

To prepare myself for battle, I spent countless hours after the girls went to bed studying and reading the Bible. At this time, I was introduced to Joyce Meyer's ministry. I did several Beth Moore Bible studies and gained perspective from those.

I listened to a Christian radio station and frequented women's conferences. There were many leaders that spoke truth and life into me during this unquenchable time in my life. I was hungry for the Word and I "tasted and saw that the Lord was good" through this season (Psalm 34:8).

Once the decision was made, I now had to figure out how to search for the parents. I made an exhaustive list of what I was looking for—things I couldn't provide—in the adoptive parents. They needed to be strong practicing Christians, have the ability for the mom to stay home, demonstrate loving kindness towards each other, have a stable income, live in Maryland, communicate well, be educated, and have a loving and caring extended family. I was only going to consider an **open adoption**, where there was free communication back and forth, where the child would know their adoptive story, and where I could eventually meet her. As part of my list, I wanted to meet the couple by visiting them in their home and see the room she would come home to. This was not typical, but there was nothing about this entire situation that was typical. I was in control. As the birth mother, it is your right and privilege to determine how the process will unfold. As the birth mother, you are in control of how the adoption agreement is drawn up. I had determined this would be a private adoption. There would be no agency involvement. But when I did some preliminary searches for adoption resources, I was disappointed to find it very limited.

With the groundwork laid, I scheduled my doctor's appointment for my first prenatal visit. The doctor ordered a blood test to confirm the pregnancy. The nurse came in, drew the blood, and left the room. While I was waiting, I felt excited, relieved, determined, and anxious all at the same time. *Was there a possibility that all the drugstore pregnancy tests were wrong?*

Women have had false positives before. It's possible mine was too, right? But I was wrong. The nurse came back in and delivered the news that I was indeed pregnant, and the doctor did an exam. Once he left the room, and while the nurse was changing the table dressing, I gently whispered (as if someone else might hear me, or her judgement might be less offensive if I whispered), "Do you have any resources or information for someone who might be considering adoption for her baby?" Of course, this was already my intention, but to spare ridicule or open rebuke and to avoid answering any uncomfortable questions I said, "might be considering."

The nurse stopped what she was doing and looked me straight in the eyes. I was apprehensive of what she might say or do (again expecting judgement or ridicule) but like trying to put toothpaste back into the tube, I could not retract my words. It seemed like I waited forever, but then her response took my breath away.

"I know someone who works at the hospital whose daughter and son-in-law have tried for five years to get pregnant naturally and two attempts at in vitro fertilization without success. They have decided to adopt," the nurse exclaimed.

What was she saying? I couldn't wrap my mind around her words. Was I hearing what God had planned long ago? I am not sure how long I was lost in my thoughts, but when I came to the nurse told me she would be right back. It was the first time in this entire journey I felt accepted. When she returned, she handed

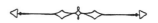

Could these be the parents the Lord said He already picked out? Does God really work like that?

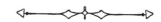

me a piece of paper with a phone number on it. This woman, Cheryl, had given the nurse permission to pass it along and added "tell her to call when or if she is ready." What a leap of faith on her part. I left the appointment a little less paralyzed by fear, and a little more drawn to hope.

I continued my routine of diving into the Word which always seemed to usher in peace. I did not seek any other options for adoptive parents. I had that piece of paper with me and pulled it out daily to make sure the number was still there. It took me six weeks before I called. By this time, I had a noticeable bump. It's not that I wasn't motivated to call, I was just gripped by the unknown. What if she didn't like me? What if they didn't meet my criteria? How would I handle it if I didn't like them? I had no back-up plan. My struggle to call Cheryl was private. I carried the weight of this decision on my own. When I finally mustered up the nerve to call, the number was disconnected! *What?* I redialed the number, only this time much slower. *Maybe I misdialed?* I dialed one more time, staring at the numbers as I pressed each one, but got the same thing "This number is no longer in service." At this moment, I was doubting that the Lord had chosen these parents. I must have been mistaken. Getting this phone number seemed too easy. I guess I had been putting all my faith into this one possibility. *Now what do I do?*

I decided to call the doctor's office and ask to speak to the nurse. I reminded her who I was and that the number I had was disconnected. She placed me on hold and came back with Cheryl's mom's number, which she knew was correct. I called immediately. Truly, this was a divine appointment. "Mom" was wonderful. She did what any mother would do and pre-screened me before passing along Cheryl's number. She had no expectations and wasn't getting her hopes up knowing this was a long shot. I didn't wait six weeks to call this time. When I called, I had my "adoptive parents' criteria" list in front of me. Our first conversation was two hours long. You could say, we hit it off. It appeared they had exactly what I was looking for to give my daughter the best life possible. When we got to the part about the home visit, Cheryl welcomed it. The home visit proved to be delightful and getting to know Cheryl and Nick made me certain they were the parents God was talking about all those weeks ago on the side of the road. Can you see how God orchestrated the turn of events? Nick and Cheryl agreed with the open adoption plan and would be involved every step of the way. Cheryl was with me on every doctor visit and when the delivery date was set, I invited her to be in the delivery room with me, and she gladly accepted.

I had a healthy pregnancy and the emotional baggage was released. When the day came for the baby's entrance into the world, I was overjoyed and saddened at the same time. But I was not prepared for what happened next. My mom, who had been absent during this season of my life, showed up at the hospital. Without being asked, Cheryl left the room to allow us privacy. (The paragraph that follows took me the longest time to write. In recalling this episode, I had an emotional breakdown. I dropped to my knees and had a good, long, hard cry.)

I didn't know how badly I had crushed my mom with my adoption decision. This was her grandchild, and I hadn't acknowledged her pain. I ignored her attempts to connect based on her earlier suggestion of abortion. Standing in front of me now, I asked her why she was here, which seemed to puzzle her, and she replied, "I want to go into the delivery room with you." "Really?" I coldly repeated back to her. "Why have you shown up now? You suggested murder!" I felt justified by my response. Was this self-preservation? How did this demonstrate my newly found faith? Why was it more important to reject her than to seek understanding, to forgive, and embrace her? I lost an opportunity here. If I had to do it all over again, my heart would be moved to compassion displaying my Father's love. It took my mom tremendous courage to show up, knowing she might be met with disgrace and rejection. On those counts, sadly, I did not disappoint.

    I was escorted to Labor and Delivery and a beautiful baby girl was born. Cheryl was by my side, comforting me, and guiding me in calmness. Choosing adoption and handing my newly delivered baby to her new parents had a great emotional impact on me. I wish I could tell you it was easy. It wasn't. But it was worth it seeing the joy on their faces as Nick and Cheryl held their daughter. It brought tears of hope and happiness to me. This little girl was where she belonged and would be given the love, opportunities, and attention she deserved. Much to my surprise, Chad showed up to hold the baby and then much to everyone's relief, he signed the papers. There were other friends and a few family members that visited that day and they were able to love on her, too. I was able to hold her, which was arranged before her birth, and love her while simultaneously saying bye, for now.

Pregnant with Harlee

Kimmie and CJ holding Harlee at the hospital.

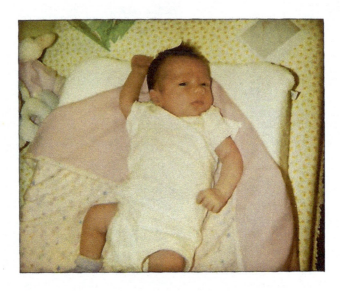

Harlee at 1 Week

I studied Harlee and once I committed her perfect features to memory, I handed her to her parents and watched them walk out the door. Although my eyes were filled with joyful tears, I was confident in knowing she was going to be given a beautiful chance at a fulfilled life, something I couldn't provide. I watched Harlee grow up over the next seventeen years through letters, phone calls, and pictures. Once when she was six years old, we all got together for a visit, my three girls, my ex-husband, Chad, Cheryl and Nick, and the newest addition to their family, Rose, who was also adopted shortly after Harlee. I was nervous on the way to meet them but felt compelled to push aside the uneasiness and instead be fully present and emotionally available to relish in the incredible opportunity to see her with her family. Words cannot express the warmth and comfort I had during this visit. It was a wonderful exchange and I can remember little Harlee's sweet voice calling to my twins, by name, and motioning for them to come play. I was at peace with my choice. The collateral blessings began to flow.

Life wasn't easy, but it was wonderful again. I felt whole. Before the birth, I explained to my daughters that mommy was having a baby for someone else whose belly was broken. To my colleagues and anyone else who was not a close family member, I was a surrogate mother because surrogacy was easier to explain to strangers than my decision for adoption. When my girls were old enough to understand, I sat them down and told them the truth behind my decision to place Harlee for adoption.

God provided a way for me to choose an open adoption plan for my child. I am not embarrassed by my decision; I speak about it openly. My passion is to counsel and educate people about adoption. Birth mothers come from an assortment of backgrounds and when they choose life by choosing adoption, they are being courageous and selfless. Demonstrating the love of the Father to their preborn child. Adoption can be a beautiful, breathtaking, life-affirming experience.

God decided in advance to adopt us into his own family by bringing us to himself through Jesus Christ. This is what he wanted to do, and it gave him great pleasure.

—Ephesians 1:5 (NLT)

Chapter 10

A Whispering Butterfly and Wind on a Buttercup

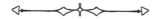

Y ou have read my adoption experience and might be wondering, as I did at the time, what an adoptive parents' journey might look like. Why do they choose to adopt? What goes into the decision? What is the whole process like? How do you make known your desire to adopt? Please allow Cheryl's transparency and vulnerability regarding her adoption journey that follows, to speak into your life and inform and broaden your understanding from the adoptive parents' perspective.

<u>Cheryl's Story</u>

Every child has her birth story. Sometimes she comes into this world after great patience, prayer, and anticipation, like a caterpillar emerging from a chrysalis as a beautiful, whispering butterfly. Other times, she comes to us like the rush of wind on a field of buttercups—unexpected, awakening, and glorious. Each gift is exactly as God meant it to be.

I grew up with a large, extended Catholic family. Each of my grandparents had several siblings, as did my parents. I am one of four children. Together our family celebrated holidays, milestones, and sacraments. I loved the buzz of big family, chatter in every room, card games, cornhole, baseball in the yard, walks, and cousins of all ages playing together. Growing up in this cacophony of family was the best. It was what I always hoped I would have when I got married. My siblings got married and started families. My story was different.

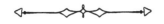

I never even remotely thought that having children would be a challenge for me.

After college and graduate school, I moved back to my hometown where my family lived. I enjoyed hanging with friends and family, trying out different jobs, dating, and pursuing hobbies. I saved money, bought a house, and built my independence. I was impatient, sarcastic, and more selfish than I care to admit. I was underwhelmed with the prospects of men. Truth be told, I had a checklist, and no one was meeting my expectations. Then God blindsided me. I fell for a man who didn't fit my "list" but was my best friend. God showed me that mature love is about loving someone's heart—their gifts and flaws, their humor, and the way they bring out the best in you. And that's what we did for each other. We realized we were in love before we even had our first kiss. We dated for a few months and got engaged. In an era of years-long engagements, our rush to the altar may have raised eyebrows. Some people may have wondered "is this a shotgun wedding? Did they rush to get married because she was pregnant?" What strange irony it would turn out to be that I couldn't get pregnant.

I was twenty-nine and he was thirty-nine. We had careers, homes, and financial stability enough to start to follow our dream of having children right away. We had discussed how we would raise our children and what our work schedules would look like. Our conversations included faith, schools, discipline, and so much more. My doctor gave us his blessing and said, "Enjoy the process (of trying to get pregnant), and if you're not pregnant in six months come see me." We were happy newlyweds and enjoyed our new life as Mr. and Mrs., but six months later, we were still not pregnant.

When we returned to the doctor, he attempted to lighten the situation by saying, "If you were sixteen and having sex in the back seat of a car, you'd be pregnant." We were referred to a specialist and learned that fertility treatments required injections, medication, temperature taking, surgical procedures, and a half-dozen doctors. It meant watching the clock and calendar, and sometimes skipping the fun spontaneity of intimacy because *science* said it was the day to have intercourse. I started trying new tricks—lay with a pillow under your hips, lay on the floor with your feet on the wall, don't exercise, jump, or run for two weeks. It all sounded stupid, but I wanted to get pregnant so badly that I was willing to try anything. After going through this routine for months, I still was not pregnant.

We pursued in vitro fertilization (IVF). Although the injections and procedures were probably much worse than I would allow myself to realize, it didn't matter because we kept our eyes on the prize—a baby! I attacked each step with dedication and totality: intense research, healthy diet, exercise, sleep, positivity, and prayer, never missing the scheduled pill or shot. I would go regularly for bloodwork, and then get the call from the nurse with directions for the next step. Each step in the process had specific timing and directions. Late one afternoon, the nurse called to say my blood test showed that I needed to take my shot by 6 p.m. My husband was at work, and I had a short window of time. My mother, who was a nurse and always willing to help was my backup, but she was at work. I couldn't give the shot to myself. I was desperate, so Mom arranged for me to go to a stranger's house, a nurse she knew who lived a few minutes away from me. Perfect! I threw modesty to the wind as I knocked on the door to a big beautiful home with a syringe and medicine in hand. My natural inhibitions were clouded by desperation. Knowing the clock was ticking, there was little time for pleasantries. She swiftly showed me to her master bathroom with kindness and professionalism in an attempt to ease my nerves and had me lean over the sink so she could deliver my shot in the butt! I was sure this crazy story would be the good luck charm to get the job done. Another waiting game, tricks and distractions, only to find out we still weren't pregnant.

With each failed month, I dreaded telling all the people who wished so much for our dream to come true, that it didn't take. **That** was harder than not being pregnant.

I often heard women say they wanted to be pregnant, but I don't recall ever thinking that. I always wanted to be a mother and was not willing to surrender that calling. The means in which motherhood came to me was irrelevant. With each unsuccessful month that passed, I dove deeper into research about adoption. I read books and articles. I talked with friends, friends of friends, doctors, adoption agencies, and lawyers. I knew it was my calling to find our child. When I suggested to my

You see, I never doubted I was called to be a mom. I always felt it was God's plan for me.

husband that we consider adoption, he was hesitant. Perhaps, he had never completely considered what adoption would be like. But God had a plan and it opened his heart.

My cousin and his wife were taking a road trip from Texas to New York to visit family and stopped to stay with us along the way. They brought with them their two boys and their own amazing adoption story. A few years earlier they had adopted a baby boy in Texas, then months later were called by the agency and told that their child had an older brother and the birth mother was placing him for adoption. They joyfully accepted the older brother into their family. From zero to two young children in a matter of months! Fast forward a few years and my cousin's wife was experiencing signs of menopause, weight gain, fatigue, etc. Come to find out -yup! She's one of the storics of women who become pregnant after adopting! What a joy, what a gift, three sons! Their visit was an inspiration and a turning point for us in our decision and hope to have children.

Another pivotal moment in our journey was when my husband and I babysat my niece for the weekend. We went all in for bottles, diapers, playtime, singing, reading, and nighttime-crib checks. At the end of the weekend, after she had gone home, we recapped all the activities and emotions. There was a time when I had to go out and my husband was caring for her alone. I asked him what that was like and he spoke with such excitement and joy. I asked him if he loved her and he replied, "So much, I'd give her a body part if she needed it." I replied, "That's what it's like to adopt a baby." From that moment, we were resolute that we would seek adoption together. Now it was time to seriously consider adoption. Fulfilling this dream of motherhood through adoption was far beyond my control.

I had more ideas than I could handle and impatiently got to work on each one. Why pursue one path and wait when you

Chasing Easy in a Life of Hard Choices

know what you want? Get to work! One approach I took was to reach out to obstetricians who didn't offer abortion services. I gave them a flier with our names, an unlisted phone number, and our plea: "Loving couple looking to adopt..."

We also visited adoption agencies, spoke to families who had adopted, and attended parent information sessions at churches and adoption agencies. We finally chose an adoption agency and got busy with the detailed process of submitting an application. We had friends, family, and even our pastor write letters on our behalf. We endured home inspections, interviews, and health exams. People came to our home to see if it met their standards for adopting a child, including flushing the toilets! We put together a photo album telling our story, we wrote a letter to prospective birth mothers, we laid our dreams out for strangers, and we hoped to be picked. Most of all, we continued to pray, "Thy will be done."

I had to put my trust in God, while placing my faith in another human to give us—strangers—the most selfless gift in the world, their baby. My daily prayer became, "Thy will be done."

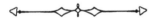

Throughout the process, so many people offered (mostly unsolicited) advice:

- Make sure you keep focusing on each other
- There are many false alarms before you find the child meant for you
- It could take years and years
- Start the adoption process, and you'll get pregnant

The ones offering the advice were not mean-spirited people, they were well meaning, but it did add a level of anxiety we didn't account for. We spent much time in prayer. I had many conversations with our lawyer and a million questions on how this process would work. We were afraid. We thought we could just adopt a baby and walk away to live our lives. We didn't think it through. We didn't consider the birth mother's perspective.

We struggled with revealing our personal information. How could we find the balance between sharing enough to connect and have a relationship and revealing too much? I had visions of a birth mother shopping in our mall or driving through our neighborhoods. I remember our attorney saying that "birth parents and adoptive parents don't often frequent the same places." I thought that was so strange, but I wanted a guarantee that backed up that statement.

Over the ensuing months we had a few calls on the unlisted landline from women with unplanned pregnancies. Sometimes they would leave a message, sometimes we would talk, but most of the time the phone never rang. We decided to cancel the unlisted phone line and just use our cell phones, which would still offer the anonymity we sought. I called on a Friday to cancel the line and was told it would be disconnected on Monday. The next Thursday, after the landline was disconnected, I got a call from my mother to come straight to her house, but she wouldn't say why. *I had never heard her like this before.* I had no idea what to expect when I ran in the door. She insisted I sit down. She couldn't organize her thoughts; her knees were shaking.

Finally, Mom told me that she had received a call from a woman who was looking for me. Her name was Teresa and her nurse had given her a flier about a couple looking to adopt.

Because the number listed on the flier had been disconnected, Teresa said she called her nurse back looking for another way to reach us. The nurse knew my mother's name and looked up her number. Teresa was clearly resourceful and determined to find us. Mom shared their conversation and punctuated it by saying that she knew right away that Teresa was a positive person and wanted a loving home for her baby. What courage it must have taken Teresa to make that call and open up to a stranger!

I grabbed the phone number and rushed out the door to my car. I couldn't wait to get home, so I immediately flipped open my phone and dialed her number. Teresa answered and proceeded to tell me the story of her pregnancy and her uncertainty. She was a few years older than me and had other children. She wanted this child to have a safe home with loving parents. One thing she said that hit me so powerfully was that **this pregnancy is no accident**. It was a consequence of actions, and therefore, she felt it was in God's plans for her to find adoptive parents.

We had a candid and easy conversation, including the reality that neither of us knew exactly what the next step would be. There was not much information available on how one goes about private adoption. She invited me to meet so we could talk more in person. I went to her place of work. It was a large office. I wore a light blue turtleneck sweater, I sat on the sofa, she sat on a chair, there were windows to my left, a door to our right. She wore a long grey skirt and had a small baby bump. We sat and chatted. *As much as I had thought about this moment, I had no plan.* She asked questions. I didn't. I didn't want to scare her away, hurt her, or ruin things. She had energy, style, confidence, and warmth. I fell for her. I remember driving home and calling my husband barely containing my excitement. All I could think was that our meeting was like going on a great blind date, you feel butterflies in your tummy and a nervous anticipation hoping they will call you again.

She did call back. She said she would love to meet my husband, and she would like to know if we would be her baby's parents. From that moment, it was now OUR baby, belonging to us all. Teresa said she wanted me to experience every part of being pregnant without actually carrying the baby. She invited me to every doctor's appointment. She told me how she was feeling. I would often make care packages of food. I made homemade soups, packed healthy snacks; I wanted to do so much more, but we had to be careful. There were laws against what adoptive parents could do for birth parents lest it be seen as "buying" a baby. How crazy is that? We couldn't do all that we wanted to for risk of getting in trouble. She was doing so much, going through so much, giving up so much, and we could do so little.

Throughout the journey, she made me feel included and accepted, and sometimes even protected. Waiting rooms became our place to talk, careful not to share too much information but enough to build our relationship. Sometimes we'd talk about others' perceptions, such as who had faith in this decision and who didn't support our plan. As we left one day and were getting on the elevator, she asked me if we wanted to know the sex of the baby. This is another example of how generous and thoughtful she was to even ask how we felt. I told her we had discussed waiting to be surprised. She shared that she thought it would be important to find out the baby's sex because it may impact the birth father's consent.

It seemed as if time stood still. Five months had passed, and it was now time for the arrival of our baby. I don't recall sleeping the night before the scheduled C-section. We rose early and headed to the hospital. When we arrived, my husband went to the waiting room, and I was taken to be with Teresa. Early on, Teresa told me she would have a scheduled C-section, and she wanted me to be in the operating room (OR) with her and welcome the baby. My husband stayed in the waiting room with Teresa's sister. When the baby was born, he was taken to the annex room off the OR. To his surprise, my mom was there too. She worked for an eye surgeon and was able to run to Labor and Delivery to be there when our baby was born.

In the operating room, I stood by Teresa's side and attempted to comfort and reassure her as she channeled her strength and courage to bring OUR baby into this world. Then, the baby girl was here, tiny and pink, wisps of soft brown hair, a button nose, and rose-colored lips tied in a bow. The four of us, Teresa, baby girl, my husband, and me, waited together in the recovery room while the staff readied the receiving rooms. My husband was holding our tiny little bundle wrapped snugly in a blanket. Teresa asked to hold her and gazed down at her lovingly. At that moment, Teresa asked us what we were naming her. Oh no! We had not made a final decision and yet here we stood in front of her. We looked at each other and whispered the name in agreement. "Harlee," we said. She gave a nod and a beautiful smile, then looked down at the sweet baby in her arms and said her name out loud.

We watched her sleeping and were awed at the miracle she was, a baby conceived unexpectedly, protected by God and her birth mother and intended for us.

Once settled in our rooms, we began the tasks of diaper changing, bottle feeding, bathing, and welcoming guests. Mostly, we just held her. We stared at her beautiful eyes, tiny pink fingers, and long toes.

A Whispering Butterfly And Wind On A Buttercup

We knew we had the most important job ever ahead of us, to love and care for this tiny child entrusted to us by God and Teresa. We brought Harlee to Teresa's room where her mother and the birth father were visiting. Then the nurses came to check on Teresa, so we went into the hall. We talked awkwardly and gave each of them time to hold Harlee. *I could feel the Holy Spirit among us.* When the nurse told Teresa's mom and the birth father they could go back into Teresa's room, Teresa's mom handed Harlee back to my husband and said, "Be a great father to her." *It was then we knew she accepted us as Harlee's parent*s.

The birth father didn't say much. But he eventually went back to Teresa's room and signed the adoption papers for the attorney. Up to this moment, we really had no idea if the adoption was going to take place. We trusted God to cover us in this situation. Teresa did not withhold the tension between her and the father, so we were prepared for the worst, which would mean leaving without our baby, and praying for the best. Ultimately our faith was in control. With the signed consent from the father in hand, we could now begin the legal part of making Harlee a permanent part of our family.

It was the day before a holiday weekend. In our state, adoptions are finalized thirty days from when the papers are filed at the courthouse. The attorneys came to the hospital to get everyone's signatures. Unexpectedly, our attorney told us that we needed to rush to the courthouse to get the papers in because the courts would be closed for the weekend and the holiday, which would add time onto our finalization. Unsure if we could get parking, we decided it was best for us both to jump in the car and rush to the courthouse. We made it within minutes of it closing and got the documents filed.

Fast forward six months. A friend was visiting from England and we were going to a new mall that was far away and taking Harlee with us. My friend had been trying to adopt at home and was having the most difficult time. She loved being with Harlee and asked so many questions. One question was what I would do if I ever ran into her birth mother. I found myself saying without hesitation, I would hug her. Hug her! If I walked in the mall and saw her, I would hug her. How far my heart had come. From fear to love.

When Harlee was a year old, we started discussing adoption again. I had always wanted a big family and knowing how hard adoption was, I wanted to get back on the list quickly. Some people speculated that adopting a second child would take four to six years. So, I pulled out the portfolio photo album that we had originally given the adoption agency two years earlier. With the help of my sister, I updated it with photos and information to include Harlee and gave it to the adoption agency to start our wait all over again. Two months to the day, I got a phone call that a birth mother had chosen our portfolio and would like to talk with us. We curbed our expectations knowing that it was unlikely that it would pan out. Even the director of the adoption agency discouraged us from getting too excited. She said it would be like lightning striking twice for a family to have two adoptions so close together. Well, lightning struck!

We were chosen to meet the baby and mother. We could barely wait. My husband was the first to hold this precious, unexpected blue-eyed baby topped off with an abundance of dark curls. We took turns rocking her in the chair and chatting with the birth mother about family, faith, hobbies, and parenting. We left uncertain, hopeful, nervous, and prayerful. Within days, the phone rang and she asked us to adopt her beautiful little girl! She told me how she felt when she went through our photo album and read our letter. The birth mother said what won her heart was the picture of our precious Harlee that was captioned, "Waiting for baby."

A whispering butterfly and wind at a buttercup. Our family of four was complete.

<u>St. Theresa's Prayer</u>
May today there be peace within you.
May you trust God that you are exactly where you are meant to be.
May you not forget the infinite possibilities that are born in faith.
May you use those gifts that you have received and pass on the love that has been given to you.
May you be content knowing that you are a child of God. Let this presence settle into your bones and allow your soul the freedom to sing, dance, praise, and love.
It is there for each and every one of us.

Chapter 11

Information Trumps Ignorance

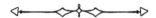

> You asked, "Who is this that obscures my plans without knowledge?" Surely, I spoke of things I did not understand, things too wonderful for me to know.
> Job 42:3 (NIV)

> Teach me knowledge and good judgment, for I trust your commands.
> Psalm 119:66

When it came to placing my child for adoption, I had to search for answers on my own. I had no idea where to look, who to ask, or what was expected of me. I didn't know what support was allowed by law and what wasn't. I recall one ignorant and misinformed person insinuating I would be paid for placing my child. In some states this may be legal, but in Maryland it was not. The audacity of that person! I was in a very tight financial situation raising three girls on my own, but the thought that I would get paid to choose adoption never crossed my mind.

There will be people, undoubtedly, who will question your motives, add doubt to your decision, or who simply want to voice an opinion. The only person I owed any explanation to was the father of my baby. My Lord and Savior knew my heart, and He is the only one that would judge my actions. He does not judge as the world does. His judgement is to decide which blessings He will extend, delay, or withhold altogether according to how I've lived my life. Did I live my life in service to Him or in service to man?

In deciding on adoption, I was motivated by love not money.

I know it would have been helpful for me at the time to get advice from women who had been in my shoes and could offer some answers, but I was too embarrassed to seek them. I decided after my experience and the emotions I went through, I wanted to *be that woman* for someone else and learn how to counsel women in unplanned pregnancy situations. So, I took a 10-week intensive training class by a licensed clinical social worker (LCSW) to be a volunteer counselor at the local pregnancy clinic.[26] After the classroom training, the next two steps were practical hands-on counseling set in the counseling room. I first observed a seasoned counselor at work, then they observed me and three months later I was approved to counsel on my own.

The training is a great resource, even if you do nothing with it. Communication, the crisis response cycle, and asking great questions were just part of the curriculum. The training is transferable to any life difficulty in marriage, work, ministry, etc., not just unplanned pregnancy. I am thankful for the opportunity this training has given me, as I have been able to share my knowledge with women who have been referred to me from friends and church leaders. In my volunteer position, I have used my personal experience with adoption to help other counselors gain knowledge and resources that would help them to become more comfortable when bridging the topic of adoption in the counseling setting. The very simple question of "Tell me what you know about adoption?" starts the discovery of where the ideas about adoption have come from and how they were formed for the client you are talking to. The follow up question is, "Who do you know that is adopted?" Questions can open up easy dialogue about the option. Even if the adopted person they know wishes they knew their birth parents, that adds to the story of how they can decide on an open adoption so their child will never have to think about who their parents were or why choosing adoption was the most loving option for them.

Thankfully the landscape of adoption has changed somewhat more favorably. There are more resources available today to help inform you; however, I wanted to spare you the awkwardness I felt at this moment of my life by offering a few answers from the voice of a practicing adoption attorney. But where would I find an attorney willing to spend some time with me sharing the process from their perspective? I knew this perspective would prove helpful and informative to anyone contemplating adoption and be a great blessing to them and me. I had many questions. Who is in control? What are the rights of each party in an adoption? What are the different types

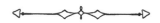

What I discovered in the counseling setting at the crisis pregnancy centers is that most people's understanding of adoption is either ill-informed or misunderstood.

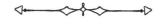

of adoption? What kind of support for the birth mother is legal? How do you best serve all parties involved?

Remember I said God knew my heart? After what I had been through, it was my heart's desire to support, equip, educate, and offer resources to women who have had an unplanned pregnancy. I wanted to be a blessing (financially and spiritually) as well. God aligned my desire with a group of women who sought after the same things. God answered my need to find an adoption attorney through a woman whom I met at church. Heather was the creator of a foundation to answer the needs of women who have chosen life and needed resources. She asked me if I would be willing to share my adoption story via video conference call and I said yes. This is how I met Sheri. God was orchestrating this divine encounter behind the scenes. Isn't that just what He does?

When you choose life, whether in parenting or adoption, you are loving your child. The only difference is that with adoption, you are loving your child into another family.

Sheri Mullikin,[27] who attended the Zoom meeting was my "in real time" answer to prayer. She is an adoption attorney who has represented both birth mothers and adoptive parents for over twelve years. Sheri is not only an adoption attorney; she and her husband also went through the process of adoption. She has a unique perspective and can counsel on both dynamics through her own personal experience. Do you see how God provided here? There are many questions, doubts, and concerns that attack your mind when considering something that you have no experience with and often aren't even sure where or how to begin. I know that's what I dealt with. I want to acknowledge that these feelings are normal.

I'm not offering legal advice here. But my prayer is that you consider Sheri's expertise below to help inform you, or someone you know, about adoption. Sheri represents both birth mothers and adoptive parents. When working with birth mothers, Sheri said they usually have already identified the adoptive family. I honestly don't know what I would have done seventeen years ago if the Lord hadn't already picked out Harlee's parents. I would have had no idea how to look for prospective parents. Today, in a social-media-saturated world, you can search for adoptive parents with the click of a button. This medium provides details on families and offers the ability to engage in person and/or virtually, which has greatly increased the success of placement. The ability to set up adoption resource pages through social networks will improve your search, whether it's for adoptive parents or placement families. Naturally you will want to exercise caution and take measures to ensure your communication is with authentic adoption-seeking parent(s).

On Sheri's site, I found this caption from the National Adoption Center:[28] **"There are no unwanted children, just unfound families."** What a beautiful reminder that God has a purpose for each child!

When representing the adoptive parents, Sheri coordinates the adoption process with the birth mother's attorney. There are some unforeseen circumstances, and some anticipated, that can change the finalization of the adoption from either side; struggles that can deter the decision: emotions, uncertainty, regret, outside influences, etc. Having an attorney that understands both sides of the equation is a bonus and affords peace amid chaos. The most common concerns for both parties surround the post-adoption contact agreement, which is enforceable by law. This agreement, as the name would imply, spells out the terms of contact agreed to by both parties. In an Open Adoption, there are many levels of contact ranging from seeing the child on birthdays and holidays to "seeing" the child through letters and pictures until the day the child reaches adulthood and can decide for themselves to meet the birth mother (as was my case). For the adoptive parents, the concern would be the birth mother ignoring her right to contact, or worse case, harassing the adoptive parents to see the child when the agreement clearly states no access.

You, as the birth mother, are in complete control of family selection, contact requirements, and the level of contact. If you are considering parenting or placing a child for adoption, I encourage you to weigh the options. Here is an exercise I did personally and used to encourage my clients in the counseling setting who were undecided, to aid and guide them in the decision-making process. Sometimes, they would complete it in front of me, and other times they would wait until they were in the privacy of their own homes. Either way, it is a revealer of your heart. I have made the resource available for counselor training and for anyone who has an opportunity to speak into someone's life to equip and educate on the option of adoption.

EXERCISE: Take out a piece of paper. On one side label the top PARENTING, and the other side label the top ADOPTION, then write down what you want for your child under the parenting label. List everything you want to provide for your child. Now go down the list and check off what you can provide. This exercise is not to shame you, but to open your mind to possibilities. Many will find that they have an impossible list and can meet the important details: food, clothing, and shelter (even if it's a struggle). Others may identify a strong preference for some desires they cannot provide: stay-at-home mom, siblings, private education, loving mother and father (many birth mothers are single), faith-based upbringing, and other opportunities. This exercise can help in the decision-making process and allows prioritization and accounting for what is most important and in the best interest of the child.

I am not downplaying the emotional component by suggesting such an exercise, I am merely approaching it from a neutral stance in order to help you inform a decision. Nothing is set in stone. The birth mother can change her mind up to thirty days after agreeing to place a child for adoption. The focus should be on the child. Understand that even those who choose to parent will admit they sometimes question their ability to do so. This is how I felt parenting my first three! There are no guarantees either way. You may find this exercise helpful, and you may discount it altogether, but I wanted to share a practical way to explore and inform your options. Ultimately, you as the birth mother, are in control.

In case you are wondering about financial support for the birth mother (Maryland, my home state is very restrictive), the adoptive parents can cover medical expenses related to the pregnancy, postpartum counseling (which in my case, I personally accepted), and legal expenses. That about sums it up. When it comes to assistance and support of the birth mother, the laws in the state of the adoptive parents, if different from the birth mother's state, will govern the legalities of the agreement. Some states are much more liberal, while others may be as restrictive as Maryland. Since it takes two to conceive, the father's rights are protected in all states to varying degrees. In Maryland, the father must agree to the adoption plan. If he is unknown, cannot be reached, or doesn't consent within the allotted time frame, the adoption can be filed. There are procedures, much too complicated for me to cover, that an adoption attorney can explain when it comes to gaining the consent of the father.

What puzzles me, and Sheri, and countless others, is that **for an *abortion* you do not have to have the consent of the father!** But when choosing life, through an adoption plan, you must have the father's consent. Do you see the injustice here? What I found interesting in talking with Sheri, is that most birth mothers decide on adoption late in the pregnancy. Why is this? Apparently, some are thought to be in denial, or pride prevents them from exploring the option to adopt, but then when the realization of parenting and raising a child sinks in, they concede that adoption is the most loving act they could choose and in the best interest of their child.

I want you to consider that when the birth mother is in Labor and Delivery, **it is OK not to answer the questions of the nurses and doctors surrounding your decision to choose an adoption plan.** Of course, you will answer a social worker, but you are not obligated in any way to respond to the inquiries of anyone else. Even the well-meaning may unintentionally say something that contradicts your decision.

I was certainly not your stereotypical birth mom and there are many others like me. Moms who already had other children and could not fathom the idea of raising another child (for varied and complex reasons). Other birth moms may be homeless, suffer from drug addictions, or they have already delivered at the hospital and decide to place their child for adoption then. Regardless of the reason behind choosing adoption, these moms need to be celebrated and recognized as courageous mommas who selflessly loved their child into the arms and home of another family. My hope is to sway the perception of adoption one life at a time.

Information Trumps Ignorance

Did you know the first recorded adoption can be found in Exodus 2:1-8? It wasn't until I experienced adoption personally that I read this account for what actually took place. Just as Moses' mom saved him, birth mothers everywhere are doing the same. I would never try to convince or coerce someone into placing their child for adoption. I merely want to share the beautiful experience that can be recognized by choosing an adoption plan.

Chapter 12

Sweet Redemption and Refreshing Restoration

Now to him who is able to do immeasurably more than all we ask or imagine, according to his power that is at work within us, to him be glory in the church and in Christ Jesus throughout all generations, for ever and ever! Amen.
Ephesians 3:20-21 (NIV)

Instead of your shame you will receive a **double portion**, and instead of disgrace you will rejoice in your inheritance. And so you will inherit a **double portion** in your land, and everlasting joy will be yours.
Isaiah 61:7 (emphasis mine)

Redemption: the action of saving or being saved from sin, error, or evil.[29]

Restoration: the action of returning something to a former owner, place, or condition.

Where am I now? I have been loved perfectly by my heavenly Father, which has helped me to love beautifully. But at the end of divorce number two, I was wondering if I would always fail at love. To avoid having to answer that question, I rejected any signs of admiration. I kept playing the movie of my life repeatedly until I was convinced to remain celibate and single for the rest of my God-given days. With my track record of failed long-term relationships and multiple divorces, there was a better than average chance it would be easy to stay single. For as far as the eye could see I was damaged goods. I didn't want to add to the rejection and abandonment I already experienced, so I avoided any advances—even simple friendly gestures. I viewed all attention as something meaningless. The Lord tells us in Romans 8:28 that he will work all things together for His good, **but no one was as bad as I was. I thought I was beyond redemption.**

God saw it all—the bad decisions, the drug and alcohol abuse, an abortion, two failed marriages, and the subpar parenting. And He still pursued me. He saw me.

God saw all my heartache, my disappointments, self-loathing, misery, and questions about purpose. He saw it all. And He still pursued me. Like the soldiers who run into battle, my Lord was running to me. Psalm 23:6 says, "Surely your goodness and unfailing love will pursue me all the days of my life, and I will live in the house of the LORD forever" (NLT). What a beautiful promise!

The song "Fully Known" by Tauren Wells[30] sums it up. The Lord ran to me instead of running away from me. He met me right where I was. None of what I was experiencing was new or foreign to Him. He was not surprised. This is the truth of a

Father who loves the unlovable, downcast, and hopeless. No earthly father could ever live up to this. My recollection of the days that led to my revelation that God loved me in my mess, didn't abandon me, and pursued me recklessly are but a blur. What I distinctly recall was what happened when He showed me true love's intention.

When I was at my lowest, the Lord took my face in his hands and gently lifted my chin and looked on me with compassion. He knew what was in store for me and how He planned to do exceedingly and abundantly more than I could ever think or imagine (Ephesians 3:20). I had given up hope and quite frankly had zero desire to ever look marriage in the face again. I was utterly destroyed. Or so I thought. But God had other plans.

I continued down the path of self-discovery. I recognized that living out of the pain that manifested from being disconnected to my Savior was taking a renegade toll on me. I had already proven that I was not worthy of a solid relationship. Negative thought patterns ruled my days stealing away any opportunity at true joy. I relegated myself to defeat, once again, and the emptiness ensued. Yes, I knew the Lord now, but it was a slow process to replace stinking thinking and hold my thoughts captive, replacing them with the promises of my creator.

Work had always been and still was my sanity. I was good at it. My work is where I felt worthy and valued. Being the manager didn't hurt either. I felt important and in control and I liked that. Pride was still a thing I struggled with. I stayed busy working, playing competitive softball, the girls were in dance and softball, and I ran the household in my spare time. I didn't really have time for a relationship. But eventually, I knew I would miss feeling wanted by someone. In an attempt to keep my sanity, I put on "man repellant" so as not to draw attention or even curiosity in my direction. I was so wounded

I didn't trust any man. I would hold anyone against my prior experiences, and I would not allow anyone to win me over. My wall was impenetrable. Life was now manageable. I was settling into my new reality and my new rhythm, being single with children. Who would want this hot mess anyway? Then it happened (and so innocently)!

Norma, a colleague turned sister from another mother, came from a large family with four sisters and two brothers. I was so much a part of the family that I was included in all the festivities which included happy birthday text strings, so when I got the call from her older brother, Ron, I was surprised but didn't think anything of it. I had always hung out with Norma's family at gatherings where I brought comic relief and coveted dance moves which made up for my lack of singing. I always felt loved and refreshed! I was able to forget my mess for a time.

It was a random phone call that would trigger the beginning of my new heaven on earth.

What impressed me the most, and still does today, is the way everyone young and old, talented, and not so much (as was my case) were part of the celebration. We would sit around and tell stories for hours, which seems to be a lost art today. Instead of inviting people over to stare at their screens, we actually put our phones down (except to take pictures) and engaged with each other. Crazy, right? When pictures and videos were captured, we'd immediately crowd around the phone of the one taking them to approve or request a new photo or video. (Of course, you know we were only looking at ourselves.) This happened every, single, time. Everyone had a role at the gatherings. The love of family and friends was evident from all the stories and laughs and the occasional tears. I loved being included. It was an escape for me. When Norma called with an invitation, I don't remember ever turning it down. The gatherings are fewer today, but the memories shared, and stories told continue to have an impact on me as it did over fifteen years ago.

While at these gatherings, I noticed Norma's brother from afar. I noticed how attentive he was to his wife of twenty-seven years, his mom, his sisters, and the kids. He was always a gentleman to everyone. I had no other thoughts at the time. I was married. He was married. That was it. He knew very little about my situation from his sister, Norma. She always honored my privacy. She was with me throughout my strained marriage all the way to the divorce I was at now, but she'd never let on the suffering I did in private. So, when Ron, three years a widower, called her to ask if I'd like a helicopter lesson for my birthday, Norma rightly answered, "Heck yes, T's fearless!" With a vote of encouragement from little sis, he decided to call me.

When I got the call, I almost ignored it; It was a number I didn't recognize. When I picked up and realized who it was, I was surprised because he had never called before. *I wonder why he's calling? Is everything ok?* I remember the sound of his voice and how well he spoke. *Okay, focus on what he's saying.* As a friendly gesture, he invited me to fly in a helicopter to celebrate my birthday. Before I could catch the words, I agreed without hesitation and exclaimed "Yes!" He made the reservation and we decided on the logistics. He knew I was having a tough time and wanted to bring some sunshine into my empty auto-pilot smiles.

I needed the release and loved the idea of flying an R22 helicopter. When the day came, I remember thinking about how patient he was because he videotaped the entire lesson. The other thing that crossed my mind was how selfless he was in this kind act that he did solely for my enjoyment. *Or did he?*

I did learn years later that this phone call that sparked a relationship was not so innocent. He confessed that he did indeed have a hidden agenda if I was receptive. *What?* We still laugh about this when we are feeling especially nostalgic.

But again, there was nothing between us. This would be the first time since I had known him (over fourteen years) that we would be alone together. That felt strange, but I quickly got over it. We were two adults just hanging out with no agenda outside of friendship. Or so I thought. This was the beginning. We had such fun we decided to hang out more often. Over the next several months, we shared different adventures: A scavenger hunt in DC (of which we were the oldest of the crew!), a motorcycle benefit ride (I rode my own) and a Mardi Gras celebration in DC, which I asked my cousin to escort me to as a chaperone and a bodyguard, because I wasn't sure if it was Ron or me that I didn't trust. LOL.

After spending a few months "hanging out," curiosity prompted me to pull out the list that I presented to the Lord after my second divorce. This list of marriage-material characteristics I wanted in a man he couldn't possibly measure up to. They were unrealistic standards. In my due diligence, I decided to cross-reference this list with what Ron appeared to possess through my observation. But after several months he consistently demonstrated these characteristics. *Could this be an act?* Remember, I was still anti-men at this point. *What was going on? Was it possible there could be more here than friendship? Could there be a budding romance? Nah.*

When I started looking forward to the phone calls and hanging out, I realized something had changed. I was also getting a little giddy and nervous with him and spent a ton of time perfecting my look, so I knew I was in trouble. *Stop. No. I don't want to. But I do want to be more than adventure buddies.* I suppressed the heart swells, but the butterflies and the smiles had a mind of their own. Ron must have had the same thing happening on his end because he made the comment, "Careful, I can be habit-forming," to which I responded brilliantly, "me too."

Could it be that my hopelessness was turning to hope? Should I trust this new revelation? My heart smiled. Could there really be another chance at love for me? After all I'd been through and all I'd done, could it really be possible? Six months into our dating, I felt I needed to spell everything out for him. That way, he could decide to walk away and the pain and recovery for me would be minimal. I wanted him to know what he was getting into. He was already aware of some of my troubles, but I chose to reveal all the drama, the scars, the bitterness, and anger I was clinging to. I revealed the heartache, most of the hidden ugliness, and the walls I built for protection. In a moment of self-preservation, I chose to take off my mask. I wanted to scare him away. But it didn't work. I had to wrestle with the feelings of insecurity and past relationship failures to see past them in order to embrace the hope of the future that God promises us in Jeremiah 29:11, "For I know the plans I have for you," declares the Lord, "plans to prosper you and not to harm you, plans to give you hope and a future" (NIV).

About a year after our first private one-on-one encounter, I presented him with another opportunity to walk away. We were sitting out back by the fire pit and I asked about his intentions and goals. What are your one-year, three-year, and five-year goals, etc. He said, "I do have a strong desire to marry." *What?* He must have known what I was *really* asking, because let's be honest, who says that? But that's exactly what I wanted to hear. My heart jumped out of my chest, but I quickly grabbed it and put it back before he could notice. I played it off. Then, the hard truth had to be reconciled. I told him that if we were not equally yoked, we could not continue. Once said, I couldn't bring the words back in. I didn't know if he would walk away or stay. It was a huge risk for me to stand on godly principles knowing that I just might lose the man I needed.

But God knew he was the right man for me. As I held my breath, Ron responded, "I am with you and it's you who has brought Jesus back into my life. You are my saving angel." You see, Ron was broken, too. He suffered a great tragedy with the loss of his wife. He was also in a place of hopelessness and had no desires or goals outside of surviving the day-to-day grind.

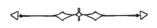

I slowly released my breath and knew that we were part of God's redemption plan for each other.

Our two shattered hearts were coming together to be a witness to the outside hurting world, demonstrating that God always has a plan. It may not be to bring fulfilment through a relationship (outside of Him), but He promises to bring you good. Clinging to that promise helped me push through the uncertainty of my future. You could say that we were both surprised by joy.[31] A joy we hadn't known in many, many years.

We decided that we did in fact want to spend the rest of our days together. Once we were aware of our future intentions, I had a simple request. I wanted him to play and sing "Marry Me" by Train[32] for the proposal. Ron is an excellent guitarist gifted with an amazing voice so I knew this would be uber romantic! He shook his head in (what I interpreted as) compliance.

We were at dinner one night, seated at a romantic table, and I thought I could pull some information out of him. I knew Ron was working on the ring design and the proposal speech.

I wanted to offer some assistance with both. Since I don't like surprises, I was feeling especially inquisitive and I asked him, "So, do you know how you're going to propose and what you'll say?" Ron responded with, "I'm working on it." *Okay, so he is open to talking about it. Cool.* I continued asking, zeroing in on what he was going to say. I can see now how my behavior must have looked. What a brat I was! How did he put up with this? He has the patience of a saint, that's how. This was my attempt at controlling the entire process because I did not like surprises. I had previously asked about the status on the ring, thinking this might be *the* dinner. When he told me it would be several weeks before it was ready, I knew in my heart this dinner date was just a dinner date. (On a side note, I also checked in his car and pockets for any sign of a ring and came up empty.) I slowly exhaled and relaxed in my seat.

While we were caught up in the moment, he reached over to his phone and started playing "Marry Me." I was totally confused. I abruptly placed my hand over his and reminded him that this song was to be played *acoustically by him* when he proposed. It was very special to me, and for the life of me, I didn't know why in the world he would be playing it now? Poor guy. I wanted him to turn it off. The waitress came by to check on us, and Ron shooed her away. *How rude. Ron is not a rude man.*

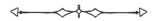

> We don't need to control everything. Letting go of control and allowing for surprises can be good for us.

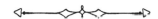

The next thing I knew, he was in front of me on one knee and before he could ask anything, I told him I wasn't prepared. *What?* In my mind I had all these ideas about how this night, when it got here, would play out. It still wasn't sinking in that he was actually proposing and not rehearsing. I must have been thinking to myself all these things when he popped the question because I didn't hear him ask me, which means I also didn't provide him an answer. When I came to my senses, he said, "You haven't answered me yet?" I immediately said, "Oh, yes! Even though you surprised me." The patrons in the restaurant clapped and we celebrated with a long embrace and, yes, with many tears on my part. Through my tears, I wanted to release the need to control everything and simply be present. I wanted to experience what Lisa Bevere talks about in her book, *Out of Control and Loving It*.[33]

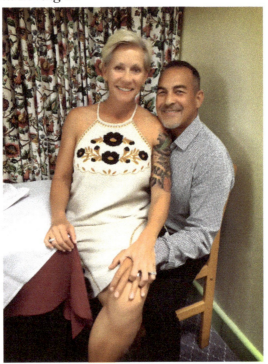

The Engagement Dinner

Pre wedding celebration

The Wedding Day

Blended family

Cousin Camp 80's theme

Sweet Redemption And Refreshing Restoration

New Years in Dover.

God knew that I needed to go through the drought in relationships in order to appreciate the amazing abundance Ron would bring. Otherwise, I could have easily overlooked him and the beautiful expression of God's love he represented. It still amazes me today how God orchestrated the entire turn of events. (Ron and I both teared up reading our story.) I pray I never grow tired of the way God saw fit to redeem both of us, especially me.

I was overjoyed and got busy with wedding plans. I thought I had 8 months to get ready, but there was yet another surprise. We lived in separate states and the government contract he was working on was not renewing. There was a new contract close to my house he was selected for, but he would not live with me unmarried. So, we did what any sound, mature, rational adults would do—we moved the date up five months! If you have ever planned a wedding, you can understand the pressure I was under to make this happen.

We decided to have the best of both worlds. We would have an immediate, private ceremony, and a celebration of marriage with family and friends on the original date five months afterwards. We got married on a Saturday on my back porch and he then moved in to start work that Monday. Where there's a will, there's an answer and a way. I think it is worth mentioning that this day almost did not happen. You see, Ron needed to have the blessing of my girls to come into my life permanently. There were two that gave immediate approval and one that hesitated. My heart sank. I knew that the outcome of my future could lay in the response of that scared and scarred eleven-year-old. Of course, I had plans to enlighten the situation if it came to that. Thankfully, it did not. He received his third and final approval to become a permanent part of our lives.

We still wanted a traditional ceremony. So, I continued with the plans and in February we had family and friends join us in the celebration. It was a beautiful night. We had decided that our story of finding love again would be an inspiration and encouragement to our guests so we each delivered a speech from our perspective to point to the unfolding of events in our lives back to Jesus. Our goal was to inject hope and inspiration to our guests. Ron and I have just celebrated our nine-year wedding anniversary. I am who I was meant to be because of the love that he has shown me. He is a God-fearing, selfless servant, and I am the recipient of that selflessness. He always claims that he is a lucky man, yet I am the one who has been double, and triple blessed because of him. I no longer see myself as damaged goods. I wish I could say that it happened overnight, but it has taken every bit of the last ten years to fully recover from who I thought I was to now focus on whose I am.

Remember not the sins of my youth and my rebellious ways; according to your love remember me, for you are good, O Lord.
Psalm 25:7 (NIV)

Our journey was not without bumps and detours along the way. The difference between going through trials and tribulations with someone who loves the Lord and loves you is the opposite of going through trials and tribulations not knowing either. I have learned to love myself. It is imperative that I share that knowledge with those I cross paths with. I may be the only one speaking life into their life. It is my duty and my obligation to share Jesus!

In case you are curious about where my girls stand with Ron today, I have to tell you that each one of them, independent of each other and on different days said the exact same thing—"Mom, I want to marry a man like Mr. Ron." As a mother, there is no greater compliment to the man you have married than that.

The Lord has given me beauty for ashes (Isaiah 61:3). I am blessed with a God-fearing, loving, nurturing husband. Yes, number three. I laid it all out for him, trying to scare him off. He didn't bat an eye. After we each suffered our own tragedy and loss, the Lord saw fit to open our hearts to love again. Letting go of the right to be angry, hurt, disconnected, and isolated led to a life of freedom from those strongholds and an openness to embrace grace and mercy. We saved each other through divine intervention. Ron supports me in every way. I feel his admiration and experience the respect of a love untainted. My girls have grown into wonderful young ladies and I am living in a home I never saw myself in, a home of contentment and godly love. The blessings are endless.

My past no longer defines me, instead it has molded and shaped me into the woman I am today. What He has done for me, He will do for you; if you let Him.

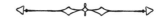

When we are at our lowest, that is when He is at our side. God will use our stories for His glory to speak life into others going through the same thing. God will use us, His servants, to bind up the broken-hearted and rescue those who are crushed in spirit. Let us not waste our instructions. I want to be used for His glory and I am excited about the next season in my life.

Chapter 13

Finishing the Work Assigned to Me

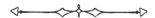

> But my life is worth nothing to me unless I use it for *finishing the work assigned me* by the Lord Jesus—the work of telling others the Good News about the wonderful grace of God. Acts 20:24
> (NLT; emphasis mine)

> Then Peter came to Jesus and asked, "Lord, how many times shall I forgive my brother or sister who sins against me? Up to seven times?" Jesus answered, "I tell you, not seven times, but seventy-seven times."
> Matthew 18:21-22

Allow me to recap what you have just read. I am twice divorced and now married to a God-fearing man. I had an abortion at fifteen. I have three daughters. My first daughter I had when I was twenty-eight and my twins when I was thirty-six. I chose an adoption plan for an unplanned pregnancy at thirty-eight from my second husband. I have shared the most intimate and vulnerable parts of my story to stretch your perception of what men and women may be going through in a similar situation. I urge you to no longer claim ignorance to the repercussions of decisions surrounding the topics of abortion, relationship warning signs, and the collateral damage or blessings that follow. It amazes me to this day, how God has used my story to allow me the opportunity to share Him.

Here is a short list of how God used me, nerves, and all, to bring glory to Him:

Six years after placing Harlee, the Lord told me to create a resource for women to understand their options when faced with an unplanned pregnancy. Option2Adopt.org was born (currently inactive).[34] I had a dream that I would travel the country speaking into the lives of junior high and high school students about their choices when it came to dating and unplanned pregnancies. This is kind of funny because, although I will do it, public speaking makes me break out in hives (sort of like working with spreadsheets does).

Well, it wasn't long after that dream that I was invited by Mike Martelli, a counsellor I met at a pregnancy clinic, to speak at an event. Careful what you dream for, right? I suppose that started the progression to public speaking. I had to lean on the Lord, and not get in the way by doing it on my own strength. I wish I could tell you I got really good at it, but that would not be the truth. I did it anyway! I am paying it forward in many ways. I have counseled at crisis pregnancy centers, trained volunteers about how to discuss adoption with pregnant women, and spoken publicly about my adoption testimony at the 40 Days for Life Campaign and the March for Life event.[35] The March for Life is an inspiring, peaceful, vibrant, and joy-filled rally of women, men, young people, and children from all across the country. Every year, tens of thousands of pro-lifers converge on the National Mall and march on Capitol Hill on the anniversary of the Supreme Court's 1973 Roe v. Wade ruling which legalized abortion in all fifty states. It's the largest annual human rights demonstration in the world.

40 Days for Life Campaign in Fullerton, MD

Speaking Opportunity

Me and Ron at a Praise n Thunder Event

Poker Run stop.

I must share the most exciting opportunity I was afforded, so far. Diane came to the pregnancy center for counseling and knew she was not going to abort. She was struggling with parenting as her boyfriend was uninvolved and she had no other support. We walked through the prospect of adoption and after many tears and considerations, she decided on placing her son for adoption and found the perfect parent. (Sound familiar?) I was able to help with the delivery of her baby boy and was blessed beyond measure to participate in the life-affirming coordination of the transfer to his parents. Diane will send me pictures now and then to see how he is growing up. It was a beautiful experience.

Most recently, I was introduced to Embrace Grace,[36] and now I lead a small group for single women who choose life for their baby. Through the covering of a church, and a twelve-week program, we offer hope, encouragement, and God's unfailing love to these women. It comes with a baby shower and princess day to boot!

I was led to write this book about my journey and to teach or preach into the lives of others based on my experiences. GRACE HAS ITS PLACE while God continues to stretch me. "But as you excel in everything—in faith, in speech, in knowledge, in all earnestness, and in our love for you—see that you excel in this act of grace also" (2 Corinthians 8:7 ESV).

In reading my story, I'm sure you can conclude that patience is not my thing. With our Western culture driven by instant gratification, is it no wonder I am bent towards that tendency? I have an excuse for everything. Once I've made up my mind about something, anyone or anything that doesn't line up with that, I will completely ignore or find support that aligns with my choice. Thank goodness the Lord understands how stubborn I am and is helping me in this area; He is far from finished with me. I imagine Him shaking His head at me, wondering how long it will take for me to "get it." I find comfort knowing He hasn't removed my picture from His fridge, either. Thank you, Jesus! My journey has allowed me to find purpose in the pain that has led to surprising and unintentional *additional* healing and restoration. Maybe that was His intention all along? I have the "beauty for ashes and dancing for mourning" syndrome now and I wouldn't change one experience that has led me to this realization.

In order to do my story justice, I had to get into character, reliving the situations and circumstances to bring to life what I was feeling and what I was grappling with. From a few of the contributors, unsolicited, raw, and real emotions surfaced. There were some buried details that the Lord revealed, and several surprising reactions that accompanied the revelations. Tears upon tears, questions, guilt, and comfort from seeing God's hands in all of it. I invite you to look for how the Lord shows up, almost like finding Waldo, in the most unlikely ways.[37] If you are like me, you may not recognize God's covering until after you have come through something. That's okay, just give Him the glory when you see it.

I believe your unique story just might help someone as I am hoping mine does for you. You might not be led to write a book, but maybe led to share your testimony to encourage others, host a blog, a podcast, or even start a ministry. Be open to the leading and be willing to bless others through it.

I spoke the following words in 2017 at my mom's funeral service with my beautiful sister by my side. These are words that I want you to take with you on your journey of healing.

Our lives are tangled together through tragedies, trials, and triumphs, which create the beautiful tapestry of our interwoven stories.

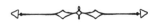

As I was getting ready for church one morning, the Lord impressed on my heart to share with you, my readers, how His amazing grace embraced my past and restored relationships that were broken, to usher in healing for all of us. Please allow my experience with a loving God to encourage you in your walk, wherever that may be.

- Mike from the aborted child: I asked him thirty-five years later how he felt about the abortion or if he ever thought about it. His reply made my mouth drop. "I think about it every day and how I would have a 30-year-old had we not done that." He was heartbroken and I never knew it!
- Divorced husband #1, Tara's dad, Luke: we were not good at marriage, but today have a healthy friendship and Tara is all the more well-adjusted as a result.
- Divorced husband #2, the twins' dad and Harlee's dad, Chad: this relationship undoubtedly was the toughest to allow grace in for healing to begin and although it took several years, we now have a healthy relationship and communicate far better today than we ever did being married.

I witness every chance I get to these men who helped shape my life today and I am thankful for the scars. God saw fit to replenish my soul and to lift my spirit through His amazing faithfulness, sacrifice, and unprecedented grace. Life is crazy good! Long ago, I heard on the radio a great quote, "If you have been wounded deeply, you will be used greatly." This is my hope for you.

But I have had God's help to this very day, and so I stand here and testify to small and great alike. —Acts 26:22a (NIV)

Mom and Dad's Wedding Day 23 Sept 1962

Over 50 years later

Finishing The Work Assigned To Me

Parpmer, Mom and Dad's Bestie

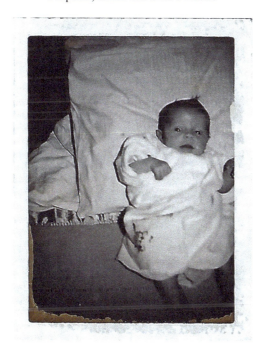

Me at 6 weeks old

Me(5YO) and Kimmie (2YO)

Me (33YO) and Tara at (5YO).

Me and Mom

Moms 70th Birthday

Besties for over 45 years: Me, Kim and Terri.

Kimmie and Keith

Family vacation in Huntington Beach, CA

Not Afraid of a Little Dirt.

Part 3

Knowledge and Perspective

Chapter 14

It's Reigning Men

> So that the man of God may be adequate, equipped for every good work.
> 2 Timothy 3:17

> But know that the Lord has set apart the godly man for Himself;
> The Lord hears when I call to Him.
> Psalm 4:3

For the women who think their past choices in men cannot be changed (which was certainly what I thought), I wanted to offer a godly man's perspective on how we can change that perception one mind at a time. I invited Mike Martelli, who has a heart of service, to share some wisdom for the women who will read this book. His desire is for the women not to compare their men negatively but to be familiar with and know how to *recognize godly characteristics in a man.* Women, we are not off the hook. We need to minister to our roles as women so that we will attract and be attracted to the right man.

Mike Martelli: What Makes a Godly Man

In 2009, Esquire magazine published an article called "What Is a Man?"[38]
The article starts like this:

> "*A man carries cash. A man looks out for those around him—woman, friend, stranger. A man can cook eggs. A man can always find something good to watch on television. A man makes things...A man can speak to dogs. A man fantasizes that kung fu lives deep inside him somewhere. A man knows how to sneak a look at cleavage and doesn't care if he gets busted once in a while.*"

Does it feel like it is hard to find a good man today? Is it any wonder that marriage rates continue to drop, divorce rates continue to rise, and nearly 40% of the children born in the U.S. today are born to unmarried women? Is it really surprising that nearly 20% of pregnancies in the U.S. are terminated through abortion? I suggest that these are not just women's issues, but that the destruction of "manhood" is actually at the root of so many of our current societal issues today. I believe we have largely lost the understanding of what it is to be a man. I submit that we have stopped teaching boys about manhood and how to become a man. In fact, I would argue that our culture has intentionally tried, and largely succeeded, to change the definition of what it even means to be a man. Not sure? Re-read the definition from Esquire magazine above.

So, what is the true definition of manhood, and where should we look for a credible source? How about the most

widely sold and read book in the world since at least 1815—
the Bible. How does the biblical definition of a man stack up
against Esquire's definition? Here are a few ways that the Bible
describes a man:

- Created in the image of God
- Warrior and protector
- In submission to God
- A student of the Word of God
- In communication with God through prayer
- Humble, selfless, and in service to others
- Honoring of God with his body

Do you see any reference to eggs, cleavage, or kung fu?

Now I know that several of these characteristics are attributable to both men and women, but they are undisputedly part of the definition of what it means to be a man according to the Bible. Do you know any men that fit this definition? If you are part of a Bible-believing church, you can probably think of a **couple**...maybe? Even within our churches today, you will be hard-pressed to find a man that checks all these boxes. I'm not talking about a "perfect man," but someone who internalizes and aspires to these goals daily. I think THAT is the real problem in today's culture. It is so hard to even find a tangible example of a godly man.

Let's talk a little more about each of these biblical characteristics of men. As I mentioned, men and women are both created in the image of God. God has both masculine and feminine characteristics. Jesus Christ is our best model for what being a man in the image of God really looks like given that He was God incarnate and a man. He was loving, compassionate, merciful, giving, and faithful. He was in submission to God the

Father, He studied the Scriptures, was in constant communication with God the Father through prayer, was humble, selfless, and pure. But He also spoke the truth in love, including the hard truth. His message of forgiveness included, "go, and sin no more". He even rebuked his friends, including Peter, when they were being selfish or primarily thinking of "human concerns."

Jesus also flipped over tables and cast out the money changers when they were defiling His Father's house. He stood in front of the prostitute when she was about to be stoned, drew a line in the sand, and challenged the religious leaders to "cast the first stone." They all walked away; no stones were cast. Men are called to be warriors and protectors. James 1:27 tells us, "Religion that God our Father accepts as pure and faultless is this: to look after orphans and widows in their distress and to keep oneself from being polluted by the world" (NIV). Proverbs 31:8 says, "Speak up for those who cannot speak for themselves; ensure justice for those being crushed" (NLT).

Yes, men are to be loving and kind and compassionate. But godly men are also called to be strong in the image of God. Not macho strong, or overbearing strong, but Holy Strong—as Jesus was strong. He stood up to the religious establishment and called us to be courageous in the face of persecution. He was even strong enough to submit to torture and death when he most certainly could have prevented it. Our culture today seems to suggest that men are either violent criminals, or pitiful, sobbing, weaklings that cower at the first sight of conflict. It almost seems as if our culture has tried to completely eliminate even the possibility of a strong, yet loving and compassionate man. Take a look at the evening news and the sitcoms on network TV today. I would suggest that the effort has been pretty successful in recent years. Can you think of a strong, loving, and compassionate man on network television today?

Another characteristic that has been all but banished from our culture is submission. We have a constant megaphone in the media shouting at us to be ourselves, express yourself, don't depend on anyone or anything, don't conform, and make your own way. While at first this message seems inspiring and encouraging, the truth is that it is a recipe for disaster and is in direct conflict with the Word of God. The Bible calls us to submit or surrender to God over one hundred times. One hundred! This does not mean hide in the corner and wait to be told what to do. This means to seek God's will every single day and try to replace your will with His will. It means to read the Scriptures, learning the lessons God has intentionally documented for us in the Bible. To be in prayer "constantly" listening for His "still small voice" to call us toward His divine plan and help us make small course corrections throughout our day.

There are thousands and thousands of self-help books and articles instructing us in all manner of things, even trying to teach us to "be the best version of yourself." I don't know about you, but if I'm trying to find Truth I'd like to go straight to the source. If I want to learn how to live my best life, I'm going to the One that created my life—the One who created ALL life! And what a bonus that He not only gave us an instruction manual in the Bible, but He also gave us a way to "phone home" and get guidance and updates any time we want—PRAYER. A real man is in the Word and in prayer **often**. When is the last time you were caught praying?

There is a natural response to submission, studying the Word, and prayer—HUMILITY. I think this is another characteristic that has been twisted by society. Humble does not mean drooped shoulders, staring at the ground, and constantly thinking and saying with a sigh, "everyone is better than me." It means that we should think of **others** before ourselves, not that others are better than us. I found a terrific quote on the website for Watermark Community Church, "Don't think less of yourself, think of yourself less." Think of yourself less—that's the key. Recognize that the world does not revolve around you, that others were not put on the earth to cater to your every whim, and, in fact, you were put here to serve others.

Men are called to be selfless and to be in service to others. The definition of selfless from Oxford Languages is: "concerned more with the needs and wishes of others than with one's own; unselfish."[39] That does not mean that men should be self-deprecating, putting themselves down, or disrespecting themselves. The Bible also teaches that Jesus died on the cross for our sins, so that we could be forgiven and spend eternity with Him in heaven. I don't think He wants us to be constantly putting ourselves down. I believe that He wants us to redirect our constant inward focus and attention outward to those around us— "think of yourself less." This constant obsession with ourselves is toxic and destructive for both men and women. You cannot be happy and selfish at the same time. Think about that.

A man is called to honor God with his body. I think a common understanding of this term is in relation to sexual purity. Paul warns us against sexual immorality over and over in his New Testament letters. The Bible is clear that sex is reserved for a man and woman who are married. That does not mean a man and a woman who are going to be married, or thinking about getting married, or anything other than ALREADY married. This encompasses all sexual activities. A man is called to be pure, sexually pure, and not to engage in sexual activity with anyone other than his wife—including himself! No, he will not die if he doesn't have sex. And no, men don't NEED it to survive. If any man suggests such a thing, run away...run far away as fast as you can (assuming this is not your husband). There are several books on this topic that can help men battle sexual addiction, and many avenues of support for men that struggle in this area. The indisputable fact remains that God calls men to be sexually pure.

But I believe that honoring God with our body extends beyond just sexual purity. Every man has God-given talents, areas of above-average capability that God blessed him with on this earth. A man may have physical talents like strength, agility, speed, etc. He may have mental talents like intellect or creativity. He may also have emotional talents like compassion or intuition (no, contrary to popular belief, intuition is not only a gift that women are blessed with). The Bible calls us to honor God with these gifts and talents and to use them for the good of others. And these "bodily gifts" are in addition to the gifts of the Holy Spirit that we are given when we submit to Christ. All of these gifts and talents are to be used to serve those around us, and ultimately draw others closer to Christ.

I have tried to describe what I see as the biblical blueprint for manhood, the ultimate goal that a godly man aspires to every day of his life. Romans 3:23 says that we are all sinners and fall short of the glory of God. So, do not expect to find a man that is perfect in all of these areas. Instead, understand that we are all *"perfectly imperfect."* There are men who strive to fulfill this biblical call to manhood. If you have a godly man, rejoice in the Lord! Thank God daily and follow your man's lead. Speak up and encourage your friends that godly men do exist and to not lose hope.

The Bible says, "Fear not," or something similar, 365 times. That is once for every day of the year. Is that a coincidence? I think not. If you are not yet married—fear not. Do not settle! Godly men are out there. Regardless of mistakes you've made in the past or where you've come from, God has a plan for you.

Trust in God and follow Him FIRST. Pray that He will send you the godly man that you've been searching for. Then have patience and trust in His timing.

If you are married and your husband does not fit this description, encourage him to become a godly man. Even if he is not a Christian, he was still created by God in the image of God, and he can become a man of God (it's already in there somewhere). This doesn't mean constantly pointing out where he doesn't measure up. Do not try to change him, and do not try to control him. But cry out to God and pray for your husband. Then share your desire to be led by a godly man.

Trust me when I say that one of the best motivators for a man is seeing the woman he loves grow in faith and relationship with Jesus.
—Mike Martelli

(Mike later shared with me the following, "I will be honest. [Writing] this was more challenging than I thought it would be. Many of these areas I have struggled with and continue to struggle with, and I must say I feel a bit hypocritical having put this all on paper for public consumption.") This admission is a true mark of a humble, godly man.

May you glean insight and your heart be encouraged to seek Him. Trust God and trust in the plan He has for you. Regardless of your romantic experience on earth, Jesus is your groom, and you will be His bride for eternity. Get close to Him now. Trust Him, and Fear Not!

Chapter 15

Silent Witnesses— The Butterfly Effect

A man of many companions may come to ruin, but there is a **friend who sticks closer than a brother**.
Proverbs 18:24 (ESV; emphasis mine)

Not only so, but we also glory in our sufferings, because we know that suffering produces perseverance; perseverance, character; and character, hope. And hope does not put us to shame, because God's love has been poured out into our hearts through the Holy Spirit, who has been given to us.
Romans 5:3–5

I felt compelled to ask a few friends for "boots on the ground" witness testimonies in hopes of once again informing you, the reader. I knew everything I did mattered and had a far-reaching impact. How can reading their perspective of my situation help you? It will likely open your eyes and your hearts to see that you are always being watched, so be mindful of what you say and do.

My friends' stories below are not to bring attention to me, but to show how God showers you with the provision you need—material provision, friendships, and support beyond all imagination. You are never alone. God is with you in the good, bad, and seemingly impossible situations. He will not abandon you when things get tough. He was with me, and He loves us all equally; He will be with you. God is love (1 John 4:8).

> I will never forsake you or abandon you. — Hebrews 13:5b

It is my hope that their stories will also enlighten your understanding of what support should look like from friends and how the God of the universe brings in the right people for your journey at just the right time! Here is what they had to say.

Mary's Perspective on the Author's Story

When I think about God and how He cares for us, the first two words that come to mind are love and selflessness. God sacrificed His only Son to save us from our sins and He selflessly pours out His love upon us. Those are two of the same qualities that I saw on display when Teresa finally came to grips with her unexpected pregnancy.

She was going through an on-again, off-again (mostly off-again) separation with her husband when she became pregnant. By the time it was confirmed, they had separated for good with no chance of reconciliation. She was left with having to support herself and her three other daughters. And now a baby?!

Her world was turned upside down. I wondered what she was going to do. I sat on the sidelines helplessly observing her struggle. While most of the people closest to Teresa were pushing for abortion, including herself, I could see the torment this was causing and how she felt trapped. She knew, even very young in her walk with the Lord, that abortion was not something that the Lord would have wanted. I remember her telling me that she was on her way to have an abortion when she had to pull her car over because she had become overwhelmed with emotion and was crying uncontrollably. She decided at that moment that abortion was not the way for her. In that moment, Teresa listened to that "still small voice," and came to terms with the idea that **the God who gives life is the only one who has the authority to take it away.**

That only left her with one option—adoption. Through her adoption decision, I saw Teresa let the agape love of God abide in her. She was willing to unselfishly give up her body, heart, and soul for what God had created through her. It was a very tough time, but I sensed that she knew she was not in this alone. She walked through this time with dignity and grace rooted in her faith and trust in God. But something else happened during that time.

God had planted another seed! You see, what the devil intends for evil, God will use for good. Reflecting on her own adoption journey, she realized a

When God calls us to do something uncomfortable, it is so He can do something remarkable! — Mary Contrino

real need for women to have access to resources that offered all the options: parenting, adoption, and abortion. Adoption, as witnessed in her own experience, was the least understood, the least accepted, and the option with the least available resources. Teresa saw this as an opportunity.

Teresa founded a website called Option2Adopt. She poured her heart into this organization and was able to help many other women that were faced with the same obstacles she faced not so long ago. See, when Teresa is in, she is ALL in! I can say that through this experience and still to this day, Teresa has stayed true to herself and her convictions while not compromising her faith.

You know, Christians often get asked, "How can you have faith or believe in something or someone you can't see?" Well, this is how we see Jesus. It is through the lives of people like Teresa who abide in the love of God and are willing to pour out that love to others even when it's uncomfortable.

Terry's Perspective on the Author's Story

I first met Teresa at church. She heard my testimony about my husband and our marital problems, about us being on the verge of divorce, and how God intervened and saved our marriage.

Anyway, back to Teresa. At first glance I thought, *this lady looks so cool with her spiked hair and tattoos*, which was quite the opposite of me. It was sort of like a blonde Pat Benatar meets Mary Poppins. However, as different as our appearances were, we had a great deal in common.

She was going through a tumultuous on-again, off-again (mostly off) marriage and we became fast friends. She joined my small church group for couples, which met off campus once a week. My husband and I agreed to counsel Teresa and her husband. We met two to three times a week. Unfortunately, after a year of trying to save the marriage, it was obvious things were not going to change and eventually the marriage failed.

As our friendship grew, Teresa shared some very personal details of her life. I remember that day very well. She said without hesitation that she and her husband had given up a child for adoption right before she and I met. She showed me pictures of Harlee and shared stories of how they stayed in touch. She was able to love her from afar. She said she had peace about the decision. I saw on her face that she made the right decision. I wanted to know more. Teresa shared how she was encouraged to abort her child. She and her husband were not together, and it looked like there was zero chance of reconciliation. Among other challenges, there were financial problems adding to the drama. While she was on her way to have the abortion, she simply could not go through with it. After pulling over to the side of the road and crying hysterically, she had a "check in her spirit" that adoption was what she needed to do.

I believe God allows you to go through circumstances so that you can share your situation and wisdom with those that need it.

Now you are probably wondering what I was thinking as she was telling me this. I did not flinch. I remember thinking I was so glad that she got that check in her spirit and opted for adoption. However, being completely honest, if she would have decided to have an abortion, I would have accepted that decision as well. I love her. But, after seeing her face light up when she showed me pictures of Harlee, I do not think she would have been at peace with a decision to abort. I believe it would have haunted her for the rest of her life.

So, where are we seventeen years later? Teresa is now helping other women by counseling them through the dilemma of an unplanned pregnancy and their options.

Teresa is doing just that. I am honored and proud to be her friend.

Me, Mary and Terry

Conclusion

A Love Letter From Your Heavenly Father

My Dearest,

I love you. I desire you. I cherish you. I have a purpose and plan for you and it is good (Jeremiah 29:11). May our time together in this life grow your trust in Me and establish new intimacy between us.

I love you unconditionally. I am faithful (1 Corinthians 1:9). I will never fail you (Psalm 136:1). I want you to understand just how I created you (Psalm 139:14)—not how the world has evaluated, labeled, or lied to you. I designed and equipped you with gifts and talents to share with the world (Romans 12:6). I created you on purpose—you are accepted and chosen (Ephesians 1:11). Like the difference in every person's fingerprint, you are unlike any other (Isaiah 64:8). You are wonderfully unique and no other person can bring what you can to the world!

You are healed! (1 Peter 2:24)
You are whole! (Colossians 2:10)
You are forgiven! (Ephesians 1:7)
You are set free! (Galatians 5:1)
You are Mine! (Isaiah 43:1)
You are deeply loved! (Ephesians 2:4)

Go forth this day knowing who you are in Me. As long as you are in relationship with Me, you will always carry peace that passes all understanding (Philippians 4:7). You are beautiful! You are My masterpiece (Ephesians 2:10 NLT).

I love you!
Your Abba Father and King
(Used with permission from Embrace Grace Inc.)

Acknowledgments

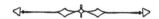

There are so many people that helped this book become reality! Forty-two years of life's stuff and the people that witnessed mine—I ask forgiveness if I leave someone out.

I want to thank my amazing husband, Ron, who put up with my moods while I worked through this project. I wanted to give up, but he reminded me why I wasn't allowed to! He is my biggest cheerleader.

I want to thank the people who contributed content to this book: Dawn S., Dawn W., Terry J., Mary C., Mike M., Dennis D., Jackie P., and Vicky E.

Thank you to my amazing editor, Gleniece Lytle. What you have done to bring this story to life is incredible! I am forever grateful, my friend.

To the FlourishWriters leaders, Mindy and Jenny, for your guidance and referrals.

Kym M. (Couture Portraits, photo credentials), Josh F. (leadership, mentorship, and guidance. I thank you for crafting the Forword), Kelly H. (mentorship, leadership, and the inspiration to coach), Terri C. and Kim Y. (every girl should have besties like you! We've had an amazing over forty-year friendship and are still going. I love you both so much), Kimmie, the most non-judgmental woman I've ever known; you've taught me so much. I love you to the moon and back, sister), and Hugh D. (who created the artwork for Option2Adopt. Thank you, brother).

I thank you, Shana! It was YOU who allowed the Lord to be a mouthpiece that started this whole thing! I also want to thank the Pregnancy Clinic Ministry, Center for Pregnancy Concerns (who started the movement over forty years ago!) Birthright Ministry, Embrace Grace, Mom and Dad, Tara, Alexa, Alyssa, Norma, Lisa B. (what a beautiful soul), Wendy A. (love your heart and unfailing encouragement!), Donna B. (the Florida respite was my beautiful beginning to serious writing!), my life coach, Barb R. (you helped me stay focused and held me accountable when I wanted to give up. Thank you!).

Thanks to all those serving on the front lines at 40 Days for Life and promoting God's grace and forgiveness in a pro-love, peaceful movement.

I thank all those who find themselves in the story, regardless of the contribution, my church family at Freedom Church in Bel Air, MD, and for all those folks who encouraged me and poured into me as I was writing.

To the Lord, my God and Savior, who saw fit to call me to write His story, may it bring You glory! And may it bring joy to the reader's heart and refresh their soul to know how much You love them. "I will sing to the Lord because he has been good to me" (Psalm 13:6 NLT).

"When you run out of words, 'I love you' is forever." — Tommy Parks (written to his wife, Jackie, before he died).

Resources

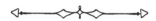

To bring awareness to you, the reader, I am listing some valuable resources that would have been helpful to me when I was considering my options. This is by no means a comprehensive list. The idea is to equip your understanding in order to make an informed decision. Please consider your local pregnancy centers and other resources to help in your decision journey.

Pregnancy/Family Support

https://aberdeenprc.org
https://bethany.org
https://cpcforhelp.org
www.optionline.org
https://pregnancyclinic.org (local to Maryland residents)

You can explore Ramah International for a list of crisis pregnancy centers near you, abortion risks, post-abortive care, and other unintended pregnancy resources. www.ramahinternational.org

Abortion

Burke, Teresa. *Forbidden Grief: The Unspoken Pain of Abortion.* Irvine, CA. Acorn Publishing, 2002

After Abortion, Hope and Healing https://afterabortion.org

See Life 2021 is a digital episodic journey that will cover topics around the pro-life movement to help educate, equip, and empower the family to #LoveEveryHeartbeat. https://www.focusonthefamily.com/see-life

Dr. Levatino, a former abortionist performing over 1200 during his practice destroys abortion in court in 2 Minutes. https://www.youtube.com/watch?v=OZXQBhTszpU

Silent No More Awareness is a resource for men seeking healing from lost fatherhood. http://www.silentnomoreawareness.org

Support After Abortion https://supportafterabortion.com

In 1994, Della Baker Hutto wrote a poem to commemorate her completion of the Bible-based study: *Forgiven and Set Free: a Post-Abortive Bible Study for Women.*
I will show loving-kindness to them and forgive their sins. I will remember their sins no more. —Hebrews 8:12 (NLT)

A Preborn Child's Conversation with His Heavenly Father

Father God, when is my mommy going to be here?

Soon, my child, soon.

Can you tell me how long?

There is no measure of time with me, my child. She is busy right now doing the work I've given her to do. When all that is done, she'll be here.

Is she going to know me when she gets here?

Yes, she will, my child, I'll let her know.

What does she look like, Father God?

Why she looks like you, my child. The same color hair, the same eyes, the same nose; you resemble her a lot.

What do you think she's going to do when she sees me?

She will run to you, take you in her arms, and love you just as any other loving Mother would do.

Father God, why has she never held me in her arms before?

She never had the chance, my child.

Why did she never have the chance, Father God?

I don't remember, my child.

> For I will be merciful to their unrighteousness, and their sins and their lawless deeds I will remember no more" —Hebrews 8:12 (NKJV)

Adoption

National Council for Adoption http://adoptioncouncil.org

Wait No More® is Focus on the Family's Foster Care and Adoption program https://www.waitnomore.org

Famous People Who've Been Adopted

Here is a short, but fascinating list I compiled of notable adoptees:

First adoption recorded in Genesis—Moses
Marilyn Monroe (actress)
Mother Teresa (humanitarian)
Michael Oher (professional football player whose story inspired the movie, *The Blind Side,* 2009)
Newt Gingrich (politician)
Faith Hill (singer)
Tim McGraw (singer)
Jesse Jackson (politician)
Augustus Caesar (emperor of Rome)
President Bill Clinton
President Gerald Ford
John Lennon (singer)
Malcolm X (human rights activist)
Nelson Mandela (human rights activist)
Edgar Allen Poe (author)
First Lady Nancy Reagan
Jesus—adopted by Joseph, the carpenter

Questions to Ask Yourself if You Are Pregnant
(or Are Flirting with the Idea of Having Sex)

(Taken from page 10, section 3, *Consider the Possibilities* Workbook from the National Council for Adoption, 2012. Reproduced with permission.)

Consider the Possibilities is a free online program designed to give professionals basic knowledge and the tools they need to understand and share the option of adoption on an equal basis with all other options. (Excerpted in part from *Is Parenting for Me Now?* Published by Loving and Caring, Inc.)

1. What do I want out of life for myself?
2. Could I handle a child and a job and/or school at the same time?
3. Have I managed school and/or job and other activities well in the past?
4. Am I ready to give up the freedom to do what I want to do when I want to do it?
5. An example of something I would have to give up by having a child with me is...
6. Am I willing to cut back on my social life and stay home while my friends go out?
7. Would I miss my free time and privacy?
8. Can I afford to support a child?
9. Do I want to raise my child in the neighborhood I am living in now?
10. How might a child interfere with my growth and personal development?
11. How would parenting a child change my educational plans?

12. Am I willing to give a great part of my life—AT LEAST 18 YEARS—to being a responsible parent?
13. Do I like doing things with children?
14. Do I want my child to be like me?
15. Do I expect a child to make my life happy?
16. When I am around small children for a while, how do I feel after being around them?
17. Am I able to give the child the love he/she needs/deserves?
18. Am I patient enough to deal with the noise, confusion, and the 24-hours-a-day responsibility of having a child?
19. What kind of time and space do I need for myself?
20. What do I do now when I am angry or upset?
21. What would I do to a child if I lost my temper or became angry?
22. What does good discipline mean to me?
23. How would I discipline a toddler?
24. Do I get along with my family?
25. How would I take care of my child's health and safety?

Adoption Knowledge and Attitude Inventory

(Taken from *Consider the Possibilities* workbook, page 3, section 2, from the National Council for Adoption, 2012. Reproduced with permission.)

Next to each number, indicate whether you believe the statement is true or false.

____ 1. Most adopted children have identity problems because they do not know their birth parents.

____ 2. The birth father should always have a say about the adoption of a child.

___3. Adoption is so painful that most women regret the choice all their lives.

___4. The rights of the birth mother should prevail over the rights of the adopting parents and the child.

___5. Pregnant women who choose adoption take the easy way out.

___6. I am satisfied with what my agency/clinic is doing to make adoption a positive option for pregnant teens and women.

___7. Only African-Americans should adopt African-American children.

___8. Adoption is not always an option because we cannot ensure that a family is available for every child.

___9. I could never carry a child to term and give it up for adoption.

___10. It is unethical for adoptive parents to pay a fee for adopting a child.

___11. Adopted children do as well or better as other children.

___12. Even If a birth mother receives counseling and other services from an adoption agency, she is not obligated to choose adoption for her child.

___13. Little information is shared about a child's background with adoptive parents.

___14. Only people who are financially well-off can adopt a child.

___15. Most adopted children have mental health problems.

___16. Adoption is usually chosen by young women who have high aspirations.

___17. A birth mother's parental rights cannot be terminated before the child's birth.

___18. No one can love a child as much as his or her birthparent.

Studies that Show the Outcomes for Pregnant Teens and Women Who Choose Adoption

(Taken from Consider the Possibilities workbook, page 17, section 2, from the National Council for Adoption, 2012. Reproduced with permission.)

Compared with unmarried mothers who parent their children, unmarried teens who place their children for adoption also:

- are more likely to finish school and obtain a higher level of education;
- attain better employment, earning more than twice the per capita income and achieving greater financial stability;
- are less likely to receive public assistance;
- are less likely to experience another out-of-wedlock pregnancy;
- are more likely to marry in the future—and when they do, are more likely to delay marriage until an older age; and
- report a high level of satisfaction with their decision for adoption.

(Donnelly and Voydanoff, 1996; Bachrach, 1992; Kalmuss, et al., 1992; McLaughlin, Mannenen, and Winges, 1988; Stolley, 1993)

In contrast, teenagers who choose to parent their children face a large number of challenges from social, financial, and emotional perspectives:

- Unmarried mothers who parent their children are more likely to repeat an out-of-wedlock pregnancy, and are also more likely to remain single and to have children who experience out-of-wedlock pregnancy (GAO report, 1998);
- Unmarried mothers who parent their children are more likely to have serious employment and financial problems (Children's Defense Fund); and
- Only 20% of unmarried mothers receive child support from the child's father (Whitehead, 1993).

In my counselor training, one of the topics covered was correct language/terms around adoption. The history behind being "put up" for adoption begins with the orphan trains that ran from the mid-1800s until the early 1900s. During this time, eastern cities were overrun with young orphans, and there were nearly 30,000 homeless, abandoned, neglected, and orphaned children in New York City alone in 1850. You can learn more here: Adoption Language, courtesy of www.adoptioncouncil.org National Council for Adoption (NCFA).

Accurate Adoption Language

Words convey important messages! Words not only convey facts; they also evoke feelings. For example, when a TV show or movie contains language about a "custody battle" between "real parents" and "other parents," this reinforces the inaccurate notion that only birth parents are real parents and that adoptive parents aren't real parents. Members of society may also wrongly conclude that all adoptions are "battles."

Accurate adoption language can stop the spread of misconceptions such as these. But using accurate language, we educate others about adoption. We choose emotionally "correct" words over emotionally laden words. We speak and write in appropriate adoption language with the hope of influencing others so that this language will someday become the norm. (Text taken from the National Council for Adoption's Infant Adoption Awareness Training Program. Used by permission.)

The charts below show the difference between old terminology and new terminology.

Appropriate Language	Inappropriate Language
Birth parent/birth mother/birth father	Real parent, natural parent
Biological parent/mother/father	Real mother/father
Birth/biological child	Own child, real child, natural child
My child	Adopted child, own child
Person who was adopted	Adoptee
Born to unmarried parents	Illegitimate
Make an adoption plan, choose adoption	Give away, place for adoption
To parent	To keep
Child in need of a family	Adoptable child, available child
Making contact with, meeting	Reunion
Parent	Adoptive parent
Child in need of adoption	An unwanted child

Court termination	Child taken away
Child who had special needs	Handicapped child, hard-to-place child
Was adopted	Is adopted
Choosing an adoption plan	Giving away your child
Finding a family to parent your child	Putting your child up for adoption
Deciding to parent the child	Keeping the baby
Confidential adoption	Closed adoption
Unplanned pregnancy	Unwanted pregnancy, unwanted child
Could not conceive/ carry pregnancy	Couldn't have children

Adoption vs. Abortion
The Similarities

Adoption	Abortion
You can pursue earlier goals and plans.	You can pursue earlier goals and plans.
You can live independently.	You can live independently.
You will not have to parent prematurely.	You will not have to parent prematurely.
You will be free from the financial burdens of parenting.	You will be free from the financial burdens of parenting.
You will avoid being forced into a hasty marriage.	You will avoid being forced into a hasty marriage.
If you are a teenager, you can resume your youthful lifestyle.	If you are a teenager, you can resume your youthful lifestyle.

Adoption vs. Abortion
The Differences

Adoption	Abortion
Your pregnancy ends with giving life.	Your pregnancy ends with death.
You can feel good and positive about your choice.	You may feel guilt and shame about your choice.
You will remember giving birth.	You will remember taking a life.
You will have plenty of time to plan you and your baby's future.	Abortion is final; you can't reverse your decision.
You can hold, name, and love your baby.	You will never know or treasure your baby.
You can have continued contact with your child.	You will miss the opportunity to see your child develop.

Adoption goes a step beyond choosing life for your baby. It is a quality-of-life decision for you and your child. (Used with permission from Bethany Christian Services' out-of-print flyer.)

About the Author

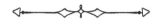

Teresa lives in Maryland with her husband, Ron. They have a blended family of five adult children, three grandchildren, and one on the way. She enjoys the "visits" with them and gets refreshed in the empty nest afterwards.

At the age of 52, she felt the Lord leading her to go back to school. She enrolled and was accepted in Emmanuel Christian Seminary in Johnson City, TN (the same town Darius Rucker sings about). She graduated with a Master of Arts in Christian Ministry in 2019, proving to herself and her daughters that it is never too late to go back to school. Her heart's desire is to serve women in many contexts based on her life experiences.

Teresa has served in the financial services industry for over twenty years, and currently runs her own financial coaching business, eLeet Financial Coaching Services www.eleetfcs.com. She takes what she learns by living it, and helps people develop plans and strategies to achieve financial wholeness/wellness.

She and her husband, Ron, serve at Freedom Church in multiple capacities.

Teresa enjoys working out, walking, and dancing like nobody's watching (but there usually is). You can catch her in the morning snuggled up with her Bible, and a good cup of joe.

She loves to learn, loves to read, and she and her husband can be found on a golf course when the weather agrees.

Endnotes

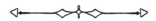

1. Here is a children's lesson on Balaam and his talking donkey that brings life to the story. https://www.youtube.com/watch?v=KG-tagFzr0k

    For other ways God shows up, I want to include the following link for your own research. It is worth listening to the message or reading what you need to get out of it. Enjoy. https://www.kevinathompson.com/god-shows-unexpected-places

2. Andrews, Andy. *The Butterfly Effect: Everything You Do Matters*. Nashville, TN: Thomas Nelson Publishers, 2010

3. There are many variations on this tale dating back to the early 1900s. https://quoteinvestigator.com/2013/12/13/pony-somewhere

4. Gold dress challenge. https://www.youtube.com/watch?v=AskAQwOBvhc

5. Gilbert, Elizabeth. *Big Magic: Creative Living Beyond Fear*. New York, NY: Penguin Publishing Group, 2016

6. Roosevelt wrote these words to his friend William Sturgis Bigelow on March 29, 1898.

7   *Unplanned.* Written and directed by Cary Solomin and Chuck Konzelman. CA., Unplanned Movie, Llc., 2019 https://www.youtube.com/watch?v=gBLWpKbC3ww

8   *Gosnell: The Trial of America's Biggest Serial Killer.* Gvn Releasing Llc., Studio City, CA. DVD, 2018 https://www.youtube.com/watch?v=ttwkr8MM9Rk

9   If you didn't know there were different types, follow this link to gain understanding. Dr. Levatino explains 1st, 2nd, and 3rd trimester abortion procedures. https://www.youtube.com/watch?v=CFZDhM5Gwhk

10 Cochrane, Linda. *Forgiven and Set Free: a Post-Abortive Bible Study for Women.* Ada, MI: Baker Books, 2015

11 Masse, Sydna. *Her Choice to Heal: Finding Spiritual and Emotional Peace.* Colorado Springs, CO: David C Cook, 2009

12 "Personhood is a [legislative] movement working to respect the God-given right to life by recognizing all human beings as persons who are 'created in the image of God' from the beginning of their biological development, without exceptions." https://rewirenewsgroup.com/legislative-tracker/law-topic/personhood/

13 *Physicians' Desk Reference.* 71st ed. Montvale, NJ: PDR Network, 2016.

14 West, Matthew. "Truth Be Told." *Brand New.* Provident Label Group LLC, A division of Sony Music Entertainment, 2019. CD

15 Post Abortive Stress Syndrome (PASS) is based on Post Traumatic Stress Disorder (PTSD). It's the name given to the psychological aftereffects of abortion. https://www.medicalnewstoday.com/articles/313098 Here is an interesting article from Iran proving that this condition is not

Endnotes

isolated to America. https://www.ncbi.nlm.nih.gov/pmc/articles/PMC6952917

16 B'More Healthy Expo is Maryland's largest health fair designed to entertain, engage, educate, and empower families to take actions and make choices to be more healthy

17 Taken from a presentation by Pam Stenzel. www.pamstenzel.com Pam Stenzel is an American speaker known for lecturing to young people about abstinence-only sex education. She has been described as "one of the country's most established abstinence-only lecturers" and speaks to more than half a million young people every year around the world. https://www.youtube.com/watch?v=qTI_38N_mZo

18 40 Days for Life is a non-stop, round-the-clock prayer vigil outside a single Planned Parenthood center or other abortion facility. It is a peaceful and educational presence. "The beginning of the end of abortion." https://www.40daysforlife.com

19 Peter Shinn is the founder and president of Pro-Life Unity and director of Cherish Life Ministries. He is also founder of ProLifeNews.tv, MonthlyCallForLife.com, and founding technical director of National Pro-Life Radio. Peter is one of the three founders of the annual Blogs4Life conference, called the Pro-Life Con which is held in Washington D.C. on the day of the annual March for Life. http://prolifeunity.com/index.php/site/petershinn

20 Smith, Ted, N. *Equal Time: An Answer Book for New Christians.* Victory Press, 1992 (Out of Print)

21 Founded in 1976, Prison Fellowship exists to serve all those affected by crime and incarceration and to see lives and communities restored in and out of prison—one transformed life at a time. Their training program

equipped me to understand how to minister to those behind bars. https://www.prisonfellowship.org

22 Christian Motorcycle Association mission is to inspire their leaders and members to be the most organized, advanced, equipped, financially stable organization, full of integrity in the motorcycling industry and the Kingdom of God. Their motto is "Changing the world one heart at a time." http://www.cmausa.org

23 Our Daily Bread Ministries, PO Box 2222, Grand Rapids, MI 49501 (616) 974-2210. These are quarterly pamphlets with multiple contributing authors.

24 Praise-n-Thunder Outreach Ministries International Incorporated, PO Box 276, Hanover, MD 21076

25 https://www.guttmacher.org/report/characteristics-us-abortion-patients-2014 Although Guttmacher is run by Planned Parenthood, I want to include this article for the one in four women in the church who've had an abortion and are too embarrassed, ashamed, and guilt-ridden to heal from it.

26 www.pregnancyclinic.org "Impossible is just an option."

27 You can peruse the link below to find answers on adoption (for Maryland) and resources to help you in this quest. http://www.mullikinlegal.com

28 The National Adoption Center creates permanent environments for children in foster care through public awareness, advocacy, and family finding. www.adopt.org

29 Taken from Oxford Languages, online https://languages.oup.com/dictionaries

30 Wells, Tauren. "Known". *Hills and Valleys*. Provident Label Group LLC, A division of Sony Music Entertainment, 2017. CD